Health in the News

RISK, REPORTING AND MEDIA INFLUENCE

ROGER HARRABIN, ANNA COOTE AND JESSICA ALLEN

King's Fund

The King's Fund is an independent charitable foundation working for better health, especially in London. We carry out research, policy analysis and development activities, working on our own, in partnerships, and through grants. We are a major resource to people working in health, offering leadership and education courses; seminars and workshops; publications; information and library services; and conference and meeting facilities.

Published by:
King's Fund
11–13 Cavendish Square
London W1G 0AN
www.kingsfund.org.uk

King's Fund charity registration number: 207401

First published 2003

ISBN 1 85717 480 1

Available from:
King's Fund Publications
11–13 Cavendish Square
London W1G 0AN
Tel: 020 7307 2591
Fax: 020 7307 2801
www.kingsfund.org.uk/publications

Cover design by Banana Design
Typeset by Grasshopper Design Company
Printed and bound in Great Britain

Contents

Section 4 The journalists' responses

Figures

Foreword

For many of us in public health it often seems that the media focus on health services – particularly their failings – drowns out all comment on health and the daily challenges we face when addressing the health needs of the population. Our experience tells us that what we have to say does not grab the headlines – despite its potential importance in improving health, preventing disease or reducing inequalities. Patterns of media reporting can influence public attitudes and behaviour as well as the priorities of policy-makers. If the biggest risks to public health are scarcely mentioned in the news while stories about NHS waiting times or health scares such as the recent SARS virus – where health risks to UK health are minimal – regularly make the headlines, it is fair to ask whether the public interest is well served by the media.

We share a belief that the media have an important role in shaping public policy but priorities differ between public health professionals and media experts. Through their study, the authors of this paper have confirmed our impressions by showing that the important – and opinion-forming – media are more interested in waiting lists and health service crises than in stories about the obesity epidemic or damage to health from alcohol or tobacco. We would, of course, want more coverage of these issues.

Equally, news reporters and editors are bound to want to set their own agenda with strong images and human interest angles. In a welfare democracy committed to social justice and equal opportunity, we all want to safeguard the freedom of the media as well as to improve health and reduce inequalities. But the first objective seems to undermine the second.

This paper highlights the need for a more informed debate about risk and ways of communicating it. The demonstration of 'deaths per story' shows that proportionally more space is given to issues which are of less importance for the population. Some of this is because it is not news, for example, that smoking kills. Unless there is a new spin, the reiteration of facts about the increasing rate of HIV/AIDS will not be of as much interest to the media as the latest failure within the health care system – but, in the longer term, prevention of the spread of disease will only be achieved through continual reinforcement of the basic messages.

Aligning the balance between public health importance and column inches or airtime is one issue. Another is to rebalance reporting to reflect the real burdens of disease, not only on human health but also on public resources, for example, by closer consideration of the ways in which mental health issues influence levels of demand for health services. While it may be reasonable for the public health experts interviewed to call for the media to take a more responsible and strategic approach to informing and educating the public, they also need to understand the culture and constraints of journalism – an issue worthy of debate.

This paper opens the way for the much needed discussion among different interest groups about how health is reported in our news media, why it matters and whether anything can be done to encourage a closer alignment between what the health statistics tell us are the biggest risk factors and the weight of news coverage.

Professor Siân Griffiths
President, Faculty of Public Health Medicine

About the authors

Roger Harrabin

Roger Harrabin is a correspondent for BBC Radio 4's *Today* programme. He is an Associate Press Fellow of Wolfson College Cambridge and Co-director of the Cambridge Environment and Media Programme, which brings journalistic decision-makers together with experts in the field of sustainable development to discuss the interplay between journalism and society. He has presented *Panorama* and *Assignment* and was founder presenter of Radio 4's *Costing the Earth*. He is married with three children.

Anna Coote

Anna Coote is Director of Health Policy at the King's Fund, London. She leads the Fund's work on health improvement, regeneration and tackling health inequalities. She was formerly Deputy Director of the Institute for Public Policy Research; advisor to the Minister for Women (1997–8); a Senior Lecturer in Media and Communications at Goldsmiths College, London University (1991–3); a producer and editor of current affairs and documentaries for Channel Four TV (1982–9); Deputy Editor of the *New Statesman* (1978–82); and a journalist and broadcaster. She is a member of the UK Sustainable Development Commission and the London Health Commission.

Jessica Allen

Dr Jessica Allen is a freelance researcher currently working for the King's Fund. She has previously worked at Unicef, New York, the American Museum of Natural History and at the London School of Economics (1994–7) researching changing media representations and understandings of crime 1945–1990. She has published several articles (with Professor Sonia Livingstone and Professor Robert Reiner) on this subject. She was awarded her doctorate at Queen Mary and Westfield College, University of London in 1994.

Acknowledgements

Many thanks to all the health professionals and journalists who made time to speak to us; also to: Baljinder Heer for her significant contribution to the research and graphics; the Reuters Foundation and Green College Oxford for hosting the project – particularly Paddy Coulter and Jenny Darnley; BBC News for funding the sabbatical and supporting the research in various ways – particularly Steve Mitchell, Kevin Marsh, Adrian van Klaveren, Bill Rogers, Sue Inglish and Richard Sambrook; Siân Griffiths, Jeremy Laurance and Jenny Kitzinger for feedback on the draft; Fred Forse for preliminary research; and Anne Lewthwaite and Sylvia Price for support. Also to William Osler, the great Oxford physician at whose desk Roger Harrabin worked, who warned his students nearly 100 years ago, 'In the life of every successful physician there comes the temptation to toy with the Delilah of the Press. There are times when she may be courted successfully but beware: sooner or later she is bound to play the harlot.'

Introduction

Anna Coote

Policy-makers are often influenced, directly or indirectly, by what they see on the television, hear on the radio and read in the general and specialist press. Members of the public may alter their behaviour in ways that affect their health at least partly as a result of information and advice they get from the media. Inevitably, then, the way stories about health are treated in the media is of interest to organisations that seek to change policy and practice in areas related to health and health care.

Background

The King's Fund is committed to improving health and reducing health inequalities. Our particular focus is on London, but most of the issues with which we are concerned affect the rest of the country too. We work across a wide spectrum, from the 'modernisation' of health and social care services to the promotion of better health for disadvantaged groups through urban regeneration. An important dimension of our 'influencing' strategy is to interest the media in our work. We find that it is infinitely more difficult to cultivate media interest in improving health and reducing health inequalities, than in, for example, 'crises' in the NHS. In fact, the media regularly come to us for contributions to stories about health services. Only rarely do they seek our help with stories about public health – that is, measures to improve health, prevent illness or reduce health inequalities. Meanwhile, unusual hazards such as the severe acute respiratory syndrome (SARS) virus, which pose relatively little danger, can occupy the headlines for weeks on end.

When Roger Harrabin, a leading correspondent with the Radio 4 *Today* programme, told us he was planning a short sabbatical to conduct a study of BBC public health coverage, it seemed a good opportunity to explore the causes and significance of the apparent imbalance in media coverage of health-related issues. We offered to support him in broadening the scope of his work. Harrabin was building on previous research he had carried out looking at media coverage of slow-moving environment stories. Support from the King's Fund enabled him to double the length of his sabbatical from three to six months. It also enabled him to test his premise – that news values tend to distort perceptions of risks to health – with a small-scale analysis of media content by Jessica Allen.

Aims of the study

The study began by exploring the views of public health experts and health policy-makers on media coverage of health issues. An analysis of news content in selected media outlets then examined news reporting of a range of health issues, including those most likely to be covered and those most closely associated with high rates of illness and premature death. Harrabin and Allen considered the balance between reporting dramatic stories such as 'crises' in the NHS and major health 'scares', and less immediately dramatic issues that statistically have a greater impact on health, such as smoking and alcohol misuse. Reporters and editors were asked for their perspectives on our research findings and on why some stories were more worthy of attention than others. Three questions lay at the heart of the inquiry: To what extent did news coverage of health-related issues reflect mortality risks shown in health data? If the balance of health news coverage was seriously out of proportion with actual risks to health, how much did that matter? Could and should anything be done about it?

To arrive at definitive answers would have been impossible in a short study. This is a highly complex field, well trodden by risk and media theorists (for example, Kitzinger 1999). We are not interested simply in accusing the media of exaggeration or misrepresentation. Nor do we wish to suggest any simple causal link between patterns of reporting on the one hand and policy decisions and personal behaviour on the other. Our modest intention has been twofold: to air a debate that has so far largely been confined to academic circles; and to raise awareness – on all sides – of the experience and views of public health experts, policy-makers, reporters and editors, along with the imperatives and constraints under which they operate. Both aims are part of a more ambitious goal, which is to shift the emphasis of the policy agenda, so that it gives higher priority than it does at present to public health targets – improving health for all and reducing health inequalities.

What did public health experts and policy-makers say?

Most public health experts and policy-makers interviewed for the study were unhappy – to a greater or lesser extent – with the way health issues were covered in the news media. All subscribed to the view that the media could exert a powerful influence over human behaviour and public policy. They argued that the news media neglected issues that were important to public health, while often giving undue prominence to issues that were less significant in health terms, including stories about the NHS 'in crisis', and that they did not always report numerical data in ways that conveyed risks accurately. Most interviewees appreciated that journalists had different priorities from those of public health protagonists, and operated under different pressures. However, they regretted a news culture that struggled to cope with complexities or long-term developments, and that did not always consider the cumulative effects on policy and practice of patterns of news reporting over time.

Most said they wanted more reporting of public health issues (such as the risks to health of smoking or obesity) to bring the balance of news coverage into closer alignment with proven health risks, although few expected any great degree of proportionality. Our interviewees called for more self-awareness on the part of the news media, and a more responsible and strategic approach to informing and educating the public, particularly from the BBC, with its unique role as public-service broadcaster. They expressed a preference for reporting by specialist journalists (who in their view had a keener understanding of the issues), less mediated by editors with different values and priorities. In common with most experts, they also wanted their own knowledge to be aired more widely and frequently in the news media.

What did we learn from the media analysis?

By conducting an analysis of health-related coverage in broadcasting and print media, we aimed to scrutinise the views of experts and policy-makers interviewed for the study. Over a year to September 2001, three BBC news programmes were studied: two on television, the *Ten O'Clock News* and *Newsnight*, and one on radio, 5 Live's news at 8.00am. This period was chosen to avoid the effects of September 11, which for a while severely disrupted patterns of reporting. The newspaper analysis took in a more recent period, October to December 2002. It included *The Guardian*, the *Daily Mirror* and the *Daily Mail*, and took account of the different patterns of coverage in news and features pages. We catalogued the numbers of stories about different health-related issues and compared the volume of reporting on specific health risks with numbers of deaths attributed to those risks. It was a limited review and should be regarded as indicative rather than definitive. We did not look at how stories were reported – for instance, how visual images and headlines were employed – nor what sources journalists used. Nevertheless, the review provided us with a useful snapshot of which issues received most attention in a selection of news outlets over a limited period of time.

In all the news outlets we studied, there was a preponderance of stories in two categories. One was the NHS – mostly stories about crises besetting the service nationally or locally, such as growing waiting times or an increased incidence of negligence. The other was health 'scares' – that is, risks to public health that were widely reported but that often involved little empirical impact on rates of illness and premature death. Themes that invariably received very little news coverage included preventive health measures and major public health risks such as smoking and alcohol, yet these tended to carry much higher health risks than NHS 'crises' and health 'scares', such as bovine spongiform encephalitis (BSE) and its human equivalent, variant Creutzfeldt-Jakob disease (vCJD) and the alleged dangers of the measles, mumps and rubella (MMR) vaccine.

Some news outlets displayed particular interests that were not reflected in others. For instance, the *Ten O'Clock News* carried a noticeably large number of stories about ethical issues in health care, such as the right to die of a terminally ill person. Some proven health risks surfaced for a limited period when 'discovered' by the media. Obesity, for example, appeared (albeit infrequently) as a news item in the papers we studied but not in the earlier period covered by the BBC research.

When we examined the newspapers, we found that coverage of public health issues was more closely aligned with proven risks than in the BBC news programmes – but only when we combined news and features pages. In other words, in the 'softer' inside pages one can sometimes read beyond the established health news agenda and find a wider variety of health-related items and much more coverage of stories about health as opposed to health services, for example, the health effects of alcohol and advice on dieting and stopping smoking. We did not study BBC features programmes, but it is fair to assume (as several of our BBC interviewees told us) that television and radio similarly deal with public health issues in magazine and documentary programmes. Features can, of course, help to inform and educate the public about health risks. However, news headlines and patterns of news coverage exert a stronger influence on public opinion and on the policy-making process, for reasons discussed in Section 3. By definition, 'news' claims to indicate what is most important and urgent.

Does it matter?

Debates about how far the media influence public attitudes and behaviour will undoubtedly continue (*see*, for example, Miller and Macintyre 1999). There are no simple rules of causality. Members of the public interpret media content in different ways, at different levels, and their interpretations vary according to the nature of the material. There are, nevertheless, at least three reasons why it may matter if the news media give a disproportionate picture of what public health experts consider to be most important and urgent in health terms.

First, there is evidence that some kinds of media coverage of some health issues make an impact on public behaviour. Take the phenomenon, not found in other countries, of parents refusing to let their children have the combined MMR vaccination after intense coverage of a lone scientific paper linking the MMR jab with autism. Arguably this is a case of media coverage affecting public behaviour in ways that may increase rather than reduce health risks.

Second, policy-makers sometimes take their cues from the media. It is not uncommon for politicians to assume (not always correctly) that the media reflect voter opinion, or prefigure it by running campaigns (with varying degrees of intensity) to influence sections of the electorate. In response, politicians issue a new promise, introduce a policy alteration, or change current priorities or spending patterns. This view was shared by our newspaper interviewees.

Third, government priorities and spending patterns influence media agendas and public attitudes in ways that are sometimes mutually reinforcing. For example, if a preponderance of news about people being kept waiting for NHS treatment prompts the Government to give higher priority to reducing waiting times, and to issue new targets on this front, it may encourage some news media to redouble their efforts to find stories about people being kept waiting. This is one way in which the media quite legitimately hold the Government to account. But the more headlines there are about waiting times, the more anxious people may become about having to wait for health services, and the more tempting it may be for the media to find stories that reflect and further feed that anxiety. Policy-makers, in turn, may come under yet more pressure to reduce waiting times. Resources may be invested accordingly – possibly at the expense of other health-related initiatives that bring greater benefit at less cost.

What do reporters and editors say?

We interviewed reporters and editors from all but one (who declined) of the media outlets in our study. Some expressed surprise at the patterns of news coverage demonstrated by our content analysis. Some said they would like to give more space to public health issues, but could not because their editors would not let them or because they could not find the 'right' stories to bring the issues to life sufficiently to win space in a crowded news bulletin. Novelty, drama and, especially for television, strong visual content were important.

Almost universally, the reporters and editors rejected the idea of 'proportionality', meaning a close match between the scale of public health risks and the weight of news reporting. Some, however, were amenable to the idea that news coverage might be more proportionate than at present. Without exception, they told us that news values were paramount – although their implicit definition of 'news' varied from one media outlet to another. In some cases, what was 'news' was what the editor considered newsworthy (and reporters tended to agree), either because it was a fresh development, or because it had already surfaced as news in other media. In others, news was partly defined by consumer preferences: whatever it took to stop people buying another paper or switching channels. News values were shaped by the priorities of the news organisation or, in the case of newspapers, its proprietor, and were further influenced by the personal interests of individual journalists.

Could things be different?

The purpose of this study is not to prescribe change but to open up a debate. Some detailed observations are set out in Section 5. Broadly, we suggest a number of developments that might encourage a closer fit between risks to public health and news reporting. We suggest there should be:

- more openness among journalists about the construction of news and its potential impact on policy-making, public opinion and behaviour
- more consistently robust handling of data analysis by news media – particularly by non-specialist journalists – in accessible terms, to help lay audiences put risks into perspective
- a better understanding among public health protagonists about how news is constructed, and the imperatives and constraints under which different news outlets operate
- greater awareness on the part of policy-makers that intense news coverage of a particular story may not necessarily reflect public opinion, nor convey an accurate picture of risks to health
- a better understanding by experts, policy-makers and media of how the public perceive and interpret health risks
- a more mature relationship between Government, experts and citizens, based on informed dialogue and mutual respect, so that risks can be discussed and negotiated openly
- stronger advocacy for public health issues at national, regional and local levels
- more debate about the role of public service broadcasters in shaping news agendas and influencing policy and practice through news reporting
- a greater readiness to track patterns of risk reporting over time
- more skilful presentation of health issues by experts and policy-makers for news and features outlets, with attention to the need for accessible language, and for sound and pictures for radio and television.

There are some positive signs. The Government is beginning to attach more importance to improving public health, rather than just improving health services. Primary care trusts are doing more to prevent illness and promote health. Efforts are being made within Government to improve the way risks are communicated. And the BBC has recently compiled draft guidance (*see* p 39) to help news reporters and editors improve their handling of risk stories. Building on these developments, we now need a vigorous public debate about health, health care, risk and reporting, about the respective roles of different news outlets in communicating health-related issues, and about how to achieve a closer match between proven health risks and news coverage without jeopardising the freedom of the media or their role in holding governments and experts to account.

1 The charge

Roger Harrabin and Jessica Allen

The greatest improvements to the health of the nation are to be gained not merely through advances in health care, but through advances in public health – measures that encourage changes in lifestyle and help to create social, economic and environmental conditions that safeguard health and prevent illness. This observation has been well rehearsed since Victorian times. Yet many public health experts say that in the news media, stories about keeping people healthy are consistently overshadowed – either by stories about alleged crises in the NHS, or by stories about health scares where the actual risk is relatively small or unproven.

Conflicting values

We conducted interviews with leading public health professionals and with health spokespeople from the three main political parties. They all independently registered the view that news media coverage of health issues appeared to be driven more by a need to entertain the public than by any desire to promote public health. A typical observation came from Dr Philip Harrison, a senior medical officer with the Medical Research Council, who told us: 'Journalists don't ask: "What is the truth?", they ask: "What is the story – how can we make this excite or disturb someone?". That is very different and, although I appreciate that they are doing their job, I do wish that it didn't have to be this way.'

Dr Harry Burns, Director of Public Health of the Greater Glasgow Health Board, told us about an exchange at a news conference called to discuss the handling of the difficult ethical issue of patients who might inadvertently have been given infected blood. A journalist wanting more information said: 'I am here to protect the public interest.' The public health doctor snapped back: 'No, I am here to protect the public interest. You are here for public entertainment.'

There was a clear discrepancy between what health experts hoped and expected from the media and how those working within the media saw themselves. (We shall hear from the journalists later – *see* Section 4.) Many of the experts and policy-makers we interviewed said they thought journalists should strive to improve society through their work and should use their valuable public platform to help promote public health. Andrew Dougal, Chief Executive of the Northern Ireland Chest, Heart and Stroke Association, asked: 'Should not the journalistic community, concerned about the common good, be motivated to report those things which might bring greatest benefit to the community, rather than those things which are most scary, pressing and revelatory?'

This expectation was particularly strong where the BBC was concerned. Given its role as public service broadcaster, the BBC was thought to carry a greater obligation than other media outlets to educate the public about their health. A senior official at the Department of Health said the BBC had a duty to educate people by seeking out news stories about proven risks like smoking. 'The BBC have a licence fee – they should deal with serious life-and-death issues... It's the BBC's duty to turn up news in the public interest, not just to report the news that is "out there".'

Questions of accuracy

Oxford epidemiologist Professor Sir Richard Doll, whose research demonstrated the link between smoking and cancer, said the media's hunger for novelty and controversy took journalists into areas of contested medical science that often unnecessarily scared the public. 'You [the media] don't like harping on about things that have been public knowledge for some time. You like things that are new. But unfortunately things that are new are often wrong, whereas things that are true take time to build up. By the time really clear evidence is available, it may no longer be interesting to the media.'

The way journalists handled statistics about risk was also a cause for concern. Professor Desmond Julian, Emeritus Professor of Cardiology, University of Newcastle, formerly President of the British Cardiac Society, cited a report that taking aspirin reduced the risk of a heart attack by 40 per cent. This sounds like a very significant reduction; however, it means that it only reduced the risk of the population suffering a heart attack from 1.2 per cent to 0.8 per cent. Professor Julian also pointed out that 'the aspirin may have increased the risk of cerebral haemorrhage by the same percentage – we simply don't know because the tests haven't been done. We have to question whether this sort of thing is worth reporting at all' (personal communication 2003; *see also* Allan 2002).

How journalists choose to represent risks in statistical terms may influence public – and professional – reactions. Risks are complex; reporting them in accessible ways can present a considerable challenge. Journalists cannot easily predict how their audiences will respond. In a psychology experiment, researchers asked psychologists and psychiatrists to judge the likelihood that a discharged mental patient would commit an act of violence. One set were told the patient had a 10 per cent chance of committing a violent act. The others were told that of every 100 such patients released, 10 would commit an act of violence. The statistic, of course, was the same. But only the latter set labelled the patient as 'likely to go crazy and kill someone' (Slovic *et al* 2000).

Influencing opinion

There was broad agreement that reporting unsubstantiated health scares could make people unduly fearful, change their behaviour in ways that might increase the risks to their health, and erode their trust in public authorities. Ragnar Lofstedt, Professor at the Centre for Risk Management at King's College, London, said he thought controversies in the media such as the MMR stories fuelled public distrust in science. 'I know that journalists have to make headlines and sell newspapers, but they should be aware of the damage this is causing to the underpinnings of trust in society.'

Hazel Blears, former Public Health minister, agreed that the media had a 'huge responsibility' in reporting health stories. 'Media scares can be so damaging to public health,' she commented. (Examples of potentially damaging consequences are discussed in Section 3.)

According to many of our interviewees, there was a danger that, if individuals or governments were encouraged to focus too much attention on unproven risks to health, they could be distracted from taking action on proven risks, such as poverty, smoking, poor housing or lack of exercise. These issues were seen as being of little interest to the media, even though they were prime determinants of health.

Dr Ian Gibson MP, Chair of the House of Commons Select Committee for Science and Technology, argued that journalists should try harder to find stories about smoking because of the need to keep its harmful effects in public view. 'The point about health messages is that you must keep reinforcing them with people, find new angles and ways of putting them across: the role of the companies, the lower-tar cigarette, advertising, genetically modified tobacco crops, and so on. Nothing stays the same and reporters should pick up on that.'

The lack of coverage of mental health stories, despite the widespread prevalence of mental health disorders, concerned many of our interviewees. 'It is almost as if it's something embarrassing that you keep hidden within the family, within the institution, within society,' Dr Gibson commented. 'Let's not talk about it, it is their own fault, let's pull together. All that prejudice comes out in the way the media cover it.'

Dr Liam Fox MP, Shadow Secretary of State for Health, said it was scandalous that mental health issues received so little coverage when they touched so many families' lives. He said attempts by his party (Conservative) to highlight mental health had been completely ignored in the media. The fears of politicians appear to be confirmed by research that shows that psychiatric illness receives much less newspaper coverage than physical illness and that the coverage it does receive is four times more likely to be negative (Lawrie 2000).

A preoccupation with the NHS

The politicians we interviewed all shared the opinion that the media should put more effort into promoting stories about health and less into highlighting unsubstantiated health hazards or the apparent failings of the NHS. Their view that the media gives a distorted impression of the degree to which the NHS was failing patients was supported by a recent poll for *The Times*. This showed that, by a three-to-one margin (64 per cent compared with 19 per cent), voters regarded the NHS as good rather than bad on the basis of their own personal experience. The margin was almost as wide on their impression of delivery of health care nationally: 57 per cent said it was 'good' compared with 22 per cent who said it was bad. In his report on the poll, Peter Riddell pointed out that personal experience of using the NHS was more positive the further one moved down the socio-economic scale. 'More than two-thirds of unskilled workers rate the NHS as good from their own experience and just one in six bad. This 70 to 17 per cent margin compares with 61 to 22 per cent among professionals' (Riddell 2003).

'Journalists are possessed by the NHS waiting lists story,' said Dr Liam Fox. 'They have little or no interest in what really matters, which is health outcomes. They insist on seeing health in terms of the NHS as a disease-response service, rather than seeing that by changing behaviour we might revolutionise health itself.'

Hazel Blears took a similar view. 'Public health in terms of protecting the people from ill-health' was rarely covered, she said. Dr Evan Harris MP, of the Liberal Democrats, told us that journalists regularly asked him to comment critically on the Government's targets on NHS waiting times. 'I always decline because I do not agree with the targets. They distort clinical priorities and lead to people who are less seriously ill being given priority over those who are in more urgent need of treatment. But this is not the comment journalists want to hear. They want to hear that the Government is failing to meet its targets. So they sometimes don't bother to use my quote on the issue.'

Patterns of news reporting that built up a picture of the NHS as perpetually crisis-ridden were thought by many of our interviewees to channel political energy and investment towards health services, at the expense of public health policies that were likely to have a greater long-term impact on health. They were seen as contributing to the public's often unjustified fear of being let down by health services, and also as prioritising curative over preventive health, in ways that distracted attention from public health messages.

Guarding the public interest

Most of the health professionals and policy-makers we interviewed acknowledged that the media were bound to have priorities and values that were different from their own. They recognised the vital role of the media in helping to hold Government to account. Some could see how experts and policy-makers themselves helped to build up patterns of news coverage by providing quotes and data. Most accepted that the impact of news reporting on public understanding and on health was sometimes positive. There was broad agreement that the spread of HIV/AIDS in the 1980s would have been much worse without the media coverage it received at the time. The media's determination to pursue the possibility of a link between BSE and vCJD was cited as another example of the media's capacity to benefit the public. On that occasion the media appear to have been right and the experts and politicians wrong, although the evidence is still disputed and the costs of avoiding risk have been queried. The Food Standards Agency recently estimated that the cost of prolonging by one year the ban on beef over 30 months old getting into the food chain is £13 billion per life saved – and they estimate 2.5 deaths from vCJD in the next 60 years (Food Standards Agency 2002).

However, some of our interviewees were concerned that HIV/AIDS had slipped from news agendas in spite of the fact that the threat was growing worldwide and even in the UK. Some also expressed a fear that the media's triumph over BSE/vCJD had led to a conviction that experts could not therefore be trusted on other health issues, and that similar examples of official failure and media success were ripe to be uncovered. This led, they felt, to potentially harmful scare-mongering over stories such as MMR.

Most made a distinction between different types of journalist. They claimed to have good working relationships with designated health and science correspondents, whom they usually considered to be well informed and mindful of the need to avoid the worst excesses of scare stories. But they were mistrustful of the propensity of editors to present issues in a sensationalist way, and of newspaper sub-editors to use inflammatory headlines and delete any content that qualified the main message. As Hazel Blears put it: 'The science correspondents and medical correspondents are on the whole extremely good – but we need to strengthen their hand because some of the more general reporting does create a real problem. That's when it all goes crazy.' Dr Harry Burns told us he had been so badly stung by radio presenters' misunderstandings in Scotland that he now refused to be interviewed on radio unless it was by a science or medical correspondent.

Conclusion

Interviewees were critical of the news media for under-reporting issues that were important to public health and over-reporting issues that were less important. They shared the view that, by generating unnecessary fears and channelling attention towards a relatively narrow illness-related agenda, the media did little to alleviate health risks and may even exacerbate them. They acknowledged that there were often sound reasons why the media behaved in this way. (The responses of news reporters and editors are set out in Section 4.)

In the next section, we consider the extent to which the complaints of public health experts and policy-makers are vindicated by actual patterns of news reporting.

2 The evidence

Are health experts and politicians justified in their criticisms of the news media? We tested their complaints with a short study of six news outlets: three key BBC news programmes and three national daily newspapers. During the course of a year, we traced health coverage on BBC television's *Ten O'Clock News* and *Newsnight*, and Radio 5 Live's *8.00am News* bulletin. Over three months, we traced health news and feature coverage in *The Guardian*, the *Daily Mail* and the *Daily Mirror* (for the methodology, *see* Appendix). Our aim was to compare the frequency of reports concerning proven public health risks (such as smoking) with the frequency of reports on newly identified, less serious risks (the MMR vaccine or BSE/vCJD). We then compared both with coverage given to stories about the NHS. It was beyond the scope of the study to explore audiences' interpretations of health stories, although we recognise that these add an important dimension to any consideration of media influence.

About the analysis

The scale of the survey was governed by the time and resources available. Our year-long analysis of the BBC ran from 10 September 2000 to 10 September 2001. This time frame was selected to avoid the aftermath of September 11, when all news output focused intensely on international events. We chose three programmes that were major flagship news outlets, each targeting a different audience. We used the BBC's electronic archive for our searches.

For the newspapers, we chose three major national dailies, each with a distinctive character and readership. We selected a more recent time frame to provide a counterpoint to the BBC period, and opted for three months rather than a year for purely practical reasons: the newspaper search was much more time consuming. We used a combination of electronic archives and – to distinguish news from features coverage – manual searches at Colindale and Islington libraries.

We covered all stories relating to health and broke these down into 19 different coding categories (*see* Appendix for details). We then combined these categories into eight groups, reflecting the aims of the study (*see* box, opposite).

CATEGORY GROUPINGS

- **Serious proven health risks**: smoking, alcohol, obesity and public health stories
- **Health scares**: BSE/vCJD, MMR
- **Health news**: stories about general illness including meningitis and tuberculosis, and male and female cancers
- **Health care stories**: NHS in crisis, negligence within the NHS, politics, NHS information, treatment and research, Harold Shipman case
- **HIV/AIDS**
- **Ethics**
- **Complementary therapies**
- **Mental health**

The first group of stories we called 'serious proven health risks', which includes the major determinants of premature death, frequently raised by our public health interviewees. This category also includes stories about public health programmes from public health bodies, such as advice on getting flu jabs. The second category is 'health scares', which covers BSE/vCJD and MMR, and other major stories about risks to health that are relatively small. The third category is 'health news', a miscellany of stories about health (as opposed to health services), such as stories about general illness, including, for example, the incidence of meningitis and tuberculosis. The fourth category is all other matters relating to health services, including 'NHS in crisis' stories. The remaining four categories, though small, seemed distinctive enough to keep separate. 'HIV/AIDS' is a significant risk to health, but not on the scale of other proven risks. 'Ethics' covers issues such as euthanasia or the implications of separating conjoined twins, which are often, but not exclusively, about health services. The last two, 'complementary therapies' and 'mental health', were kept separate because they covered both health and health care, and could not easily be absorbed into any of the other categories.

Overview of patterns of reporting health-related issues

BBC news programmes

Stories about the NHS 'in crisis' and other health service issues dominated the BBC news programmes in our survey. Stories about ethical issues made up the next largest category, followed by 'health scares'. 'Serious proven health risks' rarely made an appearance. *See* Fig 1, overleaf.

Newspaper news stories

The newspapers we studied revealed similar patterns. Between one third and one half of health-related stories were about the NHS and other health service issues. Compared with the BBC news programmes, the newspapers carried a smaller proportion of stories about health scares and ethical issues, and a higher proportion of 'health news' stories and stories about serious proven risks to health. These differences may have been partly due to the different periods covered by the two surveys (for example, the newspaper survey included the Christmas holiday period). *See* Fig 2, overleaf.

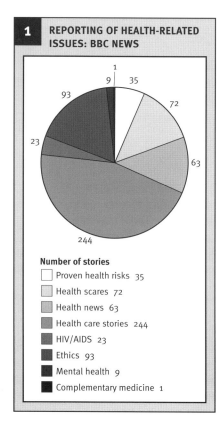

1 REPORTING OF HEALTH-RELATED ISSUES: BBC NEWS

Number of stories
- ☐ Proven health risks 35
- ☐ Health scares 72
- ☐ Health news 63
- ☐ Health care stories 244
- ☐ HIV/AIDS 23
- ☐ Ethics 93
- ☐ Mental health 9
- ☐ Complementary medicine 1

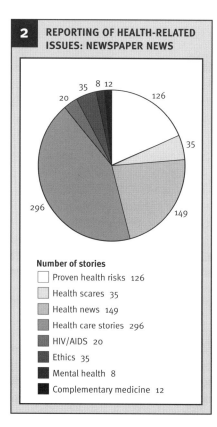

2 REPORTING OF HEALTH-RELATED ISSUES: NEWSPAPER NEWS

Number of stories
- ☐ Proven health risks 126
- ☐ Health scares 35
- ☐ Health news 149
- ☐ Health care stories 296
- ☐ HIV/AIDS 20
- ☐ Ethics 35
- ☐ Mental health 8
- ☐ Complementary medicine 12

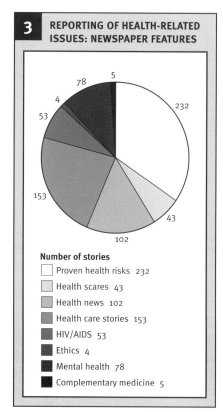

3 REPORTING OF HEALTH-RELATED ISSUES: NEWSPAPER FEATURES

Number of stories
- ☐ Proven health risks 232
- ☐ Health scares 43
- ☐ Health news 102
- ☐ Health care stories 153
- ☐ HIV/AIDS 53
- ☐ Ethics 4
- ☐ Mental health 78
- ☐ Complementary medicine 5

Newspaper features articles

Patterns of newspaper coverage altered when we considered the features pages, not just the news. Features pages often dealt with established health risks, providing information and advice. Mental health issues and HIV/AIDS were more prominent in the features pages, while stories about the NHS in crisis and other health service issues were less in evidence. *See* Fig 3, above.

'Deaths per story'

Following our analysis of story frequencies, we set out to examine any correlation between the likelihood of an issue getting in the news and the population mortality risk associated with a particular condition or behaviour. We included our major 'mortality' categories (smoking, alcohol, obesity), 'scare stories' (MMR/ measles, BSE/vCJD), HIV/AIDS and mental health. The resulting 'deaths-per-news-story chart' (opposite) is a crude measure designed to provoke debate. Put simply, it measures the number of people who have to die from a given disease to merit a story on the news. It shows that 8,571 people died from smoking for each smoking story on the BBC news. It took only 0.33 deaths from vCJD to merit a story.

Both the BBC programmes and the newspapers' news pages showed strong contrasts between the frequency of stories on a particular topic and the mortality risk associated with that condition. Reports on relatively small or unproven risks, such as BSE and MMR, vastly outweighed reports on such major killers as obesity and mental health problems.

In the features pages of the newspapers, there was a closer match between mortality risk and reporting frequency. *See* Figs 4–6, opposite.

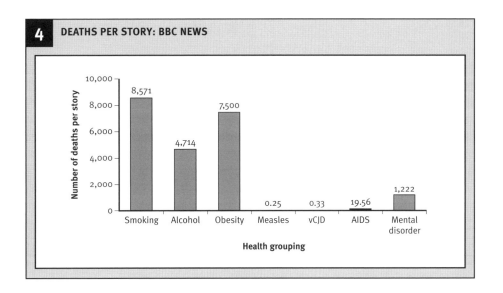

4 DEATHS PER STORY: BBC NEWS

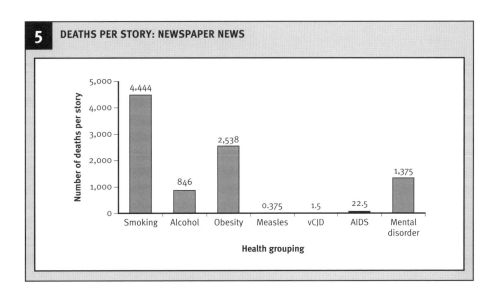

5 DEATHS PER STORY: NEWSPAPER NEWS

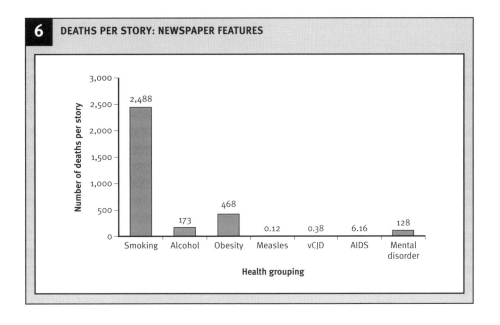

6 DEATHS PER STORY: NEWSPAPER FEATURES

Breakdown of patterns of reporting health-related issues

Our detailed analysis, comprising 19 groupings of stories for each outlet, showed that the general patterns varied according to the different media.

- In general, the BBC news programmes carried health stories that tended to cluster around a few issues: principally the NHS in crisis and negligence in the health services, BSE/vCJD, news about treatment and research, health news and stories about ethics. There were few stories about smoking, alcohol, obesity, preventive public health, mental health or complementary medicines.
- The newspaper survey revealed similar patterns in the news pages, although there were more stories concerned with public health issues and fewer on ethics.
- In the newspaper features pages, there was a far greater preponderance of stories about issues neglected by the news pages. Alcohol, obesity, mental health, and male and female cancers led the tally. Stories about the health consequences of smoking were infrequent. Similarly, stories about treatment and research, health news, and negligence in the NHS, which were much more prominent in news sections, barely surfaced at all. Figure 7 (*see* below) shows the breakdown of each medium's health reporting by percentage, for the 19 health issues. For example, 17.2 per cent of BBC news health stories focus on ethical issues, while only 1 per cent of newspaper feature articles on health focus on treatment issues.

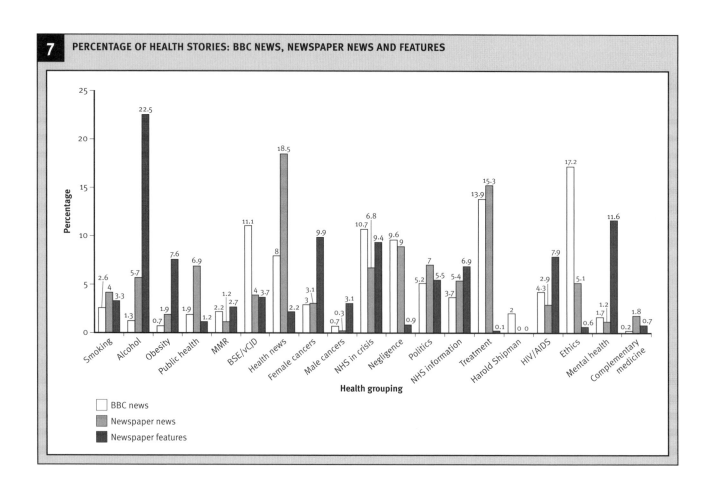

7 PERCENTAGE OF HEALTH STORIES: BBC NEWS, NEWSPAPER NEWS AND FEATURES

□ BBC news
▨ Newspaper news
■ Newspaper features

How the programmes and newspapers compare

Television and radio

BBC *Ten O'Clock News*

This programme focused strongly on ethical issues, including dilemmas about health service interventions, such as whether Diane Pretty, suffering from incurable motor neurone disease, should be allowed to die, or whether doctors should separate conjoined twins if they knew that one twin would die following the operation. These issues were evidently appealing to a programme aiming at a well-educated audience.

Another major focus was the NHS in crisis, which ran strongly throughout the year. Journalists appeared to be transfixed by the prospect of the UK's biggest public service fraying at the seams. Their interest was probably fuelled by the fact that health regularly came high on the list of public concerns, and by the Government's decision to make its impact on the NHS a yardstick for overall Government success or failure (Prime Minister's speech, 16 July 2001).

Next came BSE/vCJD – another long-running scandal that preoccupied the media after some experts raised the possibility of a huge epidemic of human disease related to 'mad cow' disease.

Those issues about which our public health interviewees had voiced most concern – smoking, alcohol, obesity and mental health – barely featured.

Newsnight

BBC television's leading nightly news and current affairs show has around one million viewers: a highbrow production, it is closely watched by the political classes. Ethical issues were dominant (though less so that on the *Ten O'Clock News*); these were followed closely by stories about BSE/vCJD and health service negligence.

The NHS-in-crisis story made only seven reports – a surprise perhaps for a programme with such an ostensible interest in politics. Mental health made four appearances (four times more than on the *Ten O'Clock News*, which carries more stories per night), smoking two appearances, alcohol one and obesity none at all.

Newsnight was found to have the most extreme 'deaths-per-story' count, resulting both from its lack of coverage of the major killers – smoking, alcohol misuse and obesity – and for its heavy coverage of minor risks, such as vCJD and the MMR vaccine.

BBC Radio 5 Live *8.00am News*

Radio 5 Live's *8.00am News* offers a lighter version of news and current affairs than Radio 4's *Today* programme. The bulletin carries fewer stories but, even so, health loomed large in 2001, with 197 stories. The category most frequently covered was treatment – information about new research and existing treatments for a variety of medical conditions. Such stories lend themselves to being told in a populist manner in a short space of time. For example, British scientists discovered a unique gene strongly linked to asthma; researchers in Southampton said it could eventually lead to a cure for the breathing disorder suffered by nearly three-and-a-half million people in the UK (Radio 5 Live *8.00am News*, 21 February 2001). Another story reported: 'An experiment in the United States, aimed at reversing the degenerative effect of Parkinson's disease on the brain, has been revealed to have disastrous side effects. The procedure involves the use of cells from aborted foetuses to try to stimulate new cell growth' (Radio 5 Live *8.00am News*, 13 March 2001).

5 Live's editors seemed to favour the NHS-in-crisis story. Ethical issues, negligence and NHS information followed. The BSE saga that so dominated the television news programmes appeared much less frequently on Radio 5. There were five stories on MMR. But 5 Live's coverage of serious proven risks to public health was more proportionate to actual health risk than the television news coverage – with eight stories on smoking, four each on alcohol and mental health, and three on obesity. *See* Fig 8, below.

8   NUMBER OF HEALTH STORIES: THE *TEN O'CLOCK NEWS*, *NEWSNIGHT* AND RADIO FIVE LIVE *8.00AM NEWS*

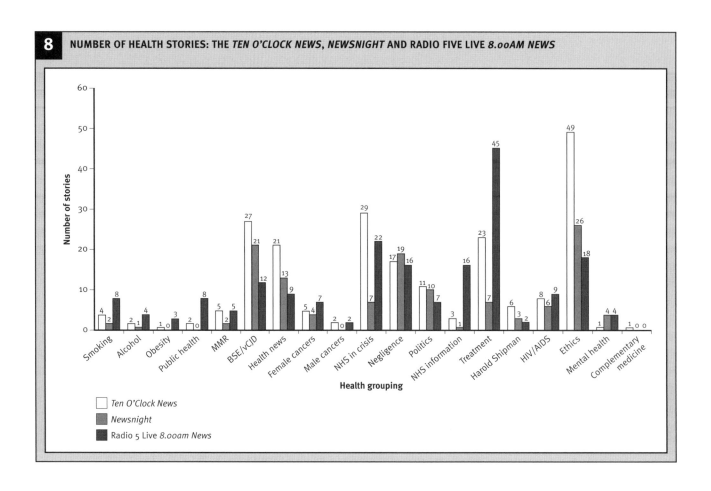

Newspaper news pages

Health news and treatment stories ran most strongly, followed by NHS-in-crisis and health service negligence stories (*see* Fig 9, overleaf). As with the BBC, much less coverage was afforded to serious proven health risks. There were 27 news stories concerned with BSE/vCJD and 20 for HIV and AIDS. MMR, perhaps a fading story by the end of 2002, generated eight news stories, as did mental health issues.

Newspaper features pages

Here the patterns of coverage changed markedly, reflecting the way newspapers tend to cover important health issues in their softer feature and lifestyle segments (*see* Fig 9, overleaf). The effects on health of alcohol was the health issue most covered in the features pages, particularly in the *Daily Mirror* (evidently related to the fact that the period covered ran up to Christmas). Next came mental health issues, particularly in *The Guardian*. Smoking was rather neglected as a health issue, even in the features pages. There was negligible coverage of stories about treatment and ethics – all covered more fully in news sections. While news and features pages covered very different health issues, together they produced a more evenly balanced pattern of coverage.

The *Daily Mirror*

The *Daily Mirror* carried a total of 98 stories about alcohol, 88 in the features sections, nearly three times that of the other two papers. There were many stories concerning cures for hangovers, how to avoid hangovers and how to control Christmas and New Year drinking. There were also numerous stories on how to cut down alcohol intake, the health effects of too much drinking, the rise in binge drinking and alcoholism, and descriptions of celebrity battles with booze.

On 10 October 2002, the *Daily Mirror* carried four stories relating to alcohol, with the following headlines:

> *Ale in a day's work: Belgo's Biermeister is paid to drink beer*
> (a humorous description of the amazing job description of the chief beer taster at London restaurant Belgo)

> *Shame of 9-yr old boozers: alarm at youth drink culture*

> *3am rehab? He's just resting his feet*
> (about actor John Thompson in rehab)

> *Girl, 8, in cider hell collapse*

Overall, the *Daily Mirror* carried fewer stories about smoking than the other two newspapers, and less than half of these were in the news pages.

The *Daily Mail*

Of the three newspapers in our study, the *Daily Mail* carried the most health stories: 493 in our 80-day period. Its main focus was the NHS in crisis. Over the study period, it ran 72 stories on this – three times more than the *Daily Mirror* and

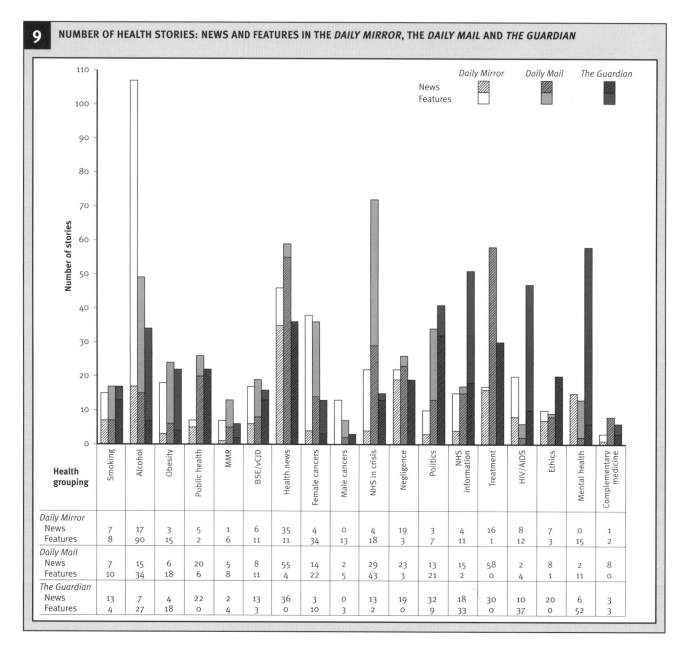

9 NUMBER OF HEALTH STORIES: NEWS AND FEATURES IN THE *DAILY MIRROR*, THE *DAILY MAIL* AND *THE GUARDIAN*

Health grouping	Smoking	Alcohol	Obesity	Public health	MMR	BSE/vCJD	Health news	Female cancers	Male cancers	NHS in crisis	Negligence	Politics	NHS information	Treatment	HIV/AIDS	Ethics	Mental health	Complementary medicine
Daily Mirror																		
News	7	17	3	5	1	6	35	4	0	4	19	3	4	16	8	7	0	1
Features	8	90	15	2	6	11	11	34	13	18	3	7	11	1	12	3	15	2
Daily Mail																		
News	7	15	6	20	5	8	55	14	2	29	23	13	15	58	2	8	2	8
Features	10	34	18	6	8	11	4	22	5	43	3	21	2	0	4	1	11	0
The Guardian																		
News	13	7	4	22	2	13	36	3	0	13	19	32	18	30	10	20	6	3
Features	4	27	18	0	4	3	0	10	3	2	0	9	33	0	37	0	52	3

nearly five times more than *The Guardian*. Although only 29 of these 72 stories were carried in the news section, the proportion of NHS-in-crisis news was still much higher than in the other two papers.

On 17 December 2002, the *Daily Mail* carried five stories and one letter about the NHS in crisis:

Health bosses quit over 'shortfall'

NHS to feel strain as heart failure cases soar

Unhealthy service (letter)

Stroke woman's cupboard ordeal

Heart attack epidemic fears

The problem: shambolic UK bores Mr Blair

> *The Guardian* carried two stories about the NHS in crisis on the same day:
>
> > *Bedside stories: The junior doctor sorts through his magazine collection and wrestles, briefly, with the thorny issue of foreign nurses*
> >
> > *Health Service failing homeless*
>
> The *Daily Mirror* had no stories.

On some days, stories carried in all three papers were framed by the *Daily Mail* as highlighting crises within the NHS, while *The Guardian* and the *Daily Mirror* took a different slant on the same story:

> **NHS-in-crisis stories, 7 December 2002**
>
> The *Daily Mail*: *Waiting lists still growing despite NHS extra billions*
>
> The *Daily Mirror*: *Waiting times down by half*
>
> The *Guardian*: *In brief: NHS nine-month list halved*

The Guardian

The Guardian had a markedly different focus from the *Daily Mail* and the *Daily Mirror* in most areas. Its coverage of mental health issues, for instance, far outweighed that of the other two papers. Overall, its most commonly reported health issue was mental health, with 58 stories. However, almost all of these (52) were carried in *Guardian Society*, a pull-out feature section for a more specialised readership. *The Guardian* ran 47 stories concerned with HIV and AIDS – more than double the *Daily Mirror* and vastly outweighing the *Daily Mail*'s six – although again, most (37) were in the features pages. *The Guardian* carried the most stories relating to health care politics (41) of which 32 were in the news section. It had the most stories based on NHS information (51) of which 18 were in the news pages. It ran 22 stories concerning public health issues, all of which were in the news section: this was three times more than the *Daily Mirror* and four stories fewer than the *Daily Mail*.

Conclusion

Our study revealed some differences in patterns of reporting between broadcast and print media, and between the individual programmes and newspapers surveyed. Nevertheless, there were significant similarities in the way all the news outlets reported health-related issues. Our findings broadly supported the observations of public health experts and policy-makers.

3 Does it matter?

The extent of media influence

Just how – and how much – the media influence and shape our lives has preoccupied media analysts for many decades. Tracing cause and effect is difficult. The connections between consuming media content, interpreting it and responding to it are highly complex and depend on the context – cultural, historical, material – in which story and audience interact.

However, there is general agreement that the media play a significant role in our lives. Professor Denis McQuail, author of the classic text *Mass Communication Theory* (McQuail 2002), identifies five functions of the mass media:
- the public's main source of essential information
- the arena where many affairs of public life are played out
- a source of definitions and images of social reality
- the place where values are constructed and expressed
- the source of a benchmark for what is normal.

This suggests that the media are important, not only in providing information, but also in shaping the way information is interpreted.

How risks are perceived

Public health doctors, government officials and scientists are trained to perceive risk as a statistical formula:

$$risk = probability\ of\ incident \times severity.$$

This is an intellectual approach based on mathematics, but recent psychological experiments suggest that the mathematical approach that underpins formal risk analysis does not come easily to those not specifically trained to use it (such as most news reporters and editors).

The experiments suggest that the human brain processes risk signals through two distinct pathways – the experiential and the analytic (Slovic 2002). The experiential system is a 'gut response'. It is intuitive, fast, mostly automatic, and relies on images and associations linked by experience to feelings. It enables us to make an instant decision on whether it is safe, say, to cross the road. The analytic system follows the scientists' intellectual approach, using formal logic, calculus and mathematical rules. It is slower and involves more effort. Thoughts are formed in words, symbols and numbers.

As journalists contend with a shrinking interest in news, they have increasingly attempted to enliven their reports by reference to personal experience – the 'human interest' angle. While print and radio reporters strive to evoke powerful images in their audiences' minds, television reporters seek out the strongest visual images and write commentary to fit. Thus all mainstream reporting – and television in particular – is inherently geared towards the intuitive system of processing risk.

A diligent correspondent may be mindful of the need to balance the emotional impact of dramatic images with careful statistics or with disclaimers about the time it will take to establish scientific certainty on a given risk. But this may have a limited impact on the audience, as strong visual images, human interest stories and the sense of immediacy inherent in a TV news bulletin drown out the effects of the balancing commentary. Viewers watching the news and even looking at pictures in the papers are readily affected by visual imagery. A TV news report, for instance on MMR, containing evocative images of autistic children, may leave a more lasting impression on the viewers' minds of the dangers of the vaccine, than a carefully worded, circumspect report, complete with scientific data, that points to its relative safety.

Risk theorist Paul Slovic warns that people's brains are badly tuned to receiving statistics unless they carry an emotional charge. 'We cannot assume that an intelligent person can understand the meaning of even the simplest of numbers such as numbers of lives at risk, not to mention more esoteric statistics pertaining to risk, unless these numbers are infused with affect [emotion]' (Slovic *et al* 2002).

Risk theories provide useful pointers for journalists and public health professionals alike. For example, a number of studies suggest that some risks trigger more alarm, anxiety or outrage than others, regardless of scientific evidence of their seriousness (Bennett 1999; Frewer 1999). Individuals find it relatively easy to judge directly perceptible risks, such as those involved in climbing a tree or driving a car (Kitzinger 1999). It is harder when the risks are perceptible only with the help of science, such as those posed by infectious diseases, and extremely hard when it comes to the risks that are 'virtual' and risks about which scientists do not agree, such as those posed by genetic engineering, climate change and various suspected carcinogens.

Furthermore, risk is not static but reflexive (Adams 1995). If the media identify a risk, the level of that risk changes as people modify their behaviour to avoid it. This type of risk avoidance can itself lead to a corresponding increase in other risks, for example, when parents worried about child abduction or road traffic keep their children indoors, contributing to decreasing levels of physical exercise among the young and increasing levels of obesity, a serious risk to child health.

Influencing public behaviour

In his recent work *Media and Health*, Clive Seale, Professor of Sociology at Goldsmith's College, traces complaints about distortion of risk by the media and lack of interest in public health over several decades. 'It has become increasingly clear to me', he says, 'that people's responses to illness, health care and health-related behaviour generally are profoundly influenced by mass media representations. This ... has been inadequately recognised' (Seale 2002).

He reports, for example, that fears in 1983 about the safety of the contraceptive pill, widely reported in the media, led to a 14 per cent drop in prescriptions for the pill and a rise in the abortion rate in the 15–19 age group in England and Wales, from 17.6 per 1,000 women (35,318 in total) in 1983 to 19 per 1,000 women (37,572) in 1984 (Wellings and Kane 1999).

A more recent study showed that a media-fuelled panic about another type of contraceptive pill in 1995, following a Government warning that pills containing a particular combination of hormones carried an increased risk of thromboembolism, persuaded some women to stop taking that type of pill (Furedi and Furedi 1996). The study blamed the Government for clumsily initiating the scare, but concluded also that the way the media reported the story helped to promote the scare. Closer inspection of the risks of the new pill would have revealed that pregnancy itself was twice as likely to trigger a thromboembolism as taking the new pill, and that giving birth or having an abortion both involved higher levels of risk. Did journalists have a responsibility to check the science, rather than just raising the alarm on the basis of the Government's warning? News of the scare appeared to influence public behaviour: the number of pregnancies rose and terminations increased by more than eight per cent that year (Office for National Statistics 1997; Wood *et al* 1997).

The MMR story offers a further example of a media-led campaign designed to reduce one risk leading to an increase in another – arguably more serious – risk. The possible risk identified in a scientific paper by Andrew Wakefield (Wakefield *et al* 1998), and widely reported in the media, was that the combined vaccination might cause autism and bowel disease in some children. It caused considerable alarm among parents and many decided not to have their children vaccinated. Take-up of the MMR vaccination declined by up to eight per cent in England between 1995/6 and 2001/2 (Office for National Statistics 2002). The effect was that an estimated 468,000 children aged between one and four had not been vaccinated against measles by 2001/2. It is impossible to estimate the number of deaths that will result, but a substantial reduction in 'community immunity' would lead to vulnerable individuals, such as children under one and people with deficient immune systems, being at greater risk. Before the introduction of the measles vaccine in 1968 there were up to 800,000 cases of measles a year, causing more than 100 deaths in a bad year. One in 15 notified cases of measles result in serious complications. Between one in 2,500 and one in 5,000 notified cases result in death (Butler 2002).

Conventions of news reporting, especially in broadcasting, favour the juxtaposition of opposing views, typically from two 'experts' who are invited to put their side of the argument. This format gives an impression of 'balance' that may not reflect the weight of evidence. A recent survey carried out for the Economic and Social Research Council (ESRC) showed that although almost all scientific experts rejected the claim of a link between the MMR vaccine and autism, 53 per cent of those surveyed when media coverage was at its height assumed that because both sides of the debate received equal media coverage, there must be equal evidence for each. Only 23 per cent were aware that the bulk of evidence favoured supporters of the vaccine (Hargreaves *et al* 2003). As Professor Justin Lewis, one of the authors of the ESRC report, said: 'The survey confirms that the news media play a key role in informing the way people understand issues such as the controversy around MMR ... While Wakefield's claims are of legitimate public interest, our report shows that research questioning the safety of something that is widely used should be approached with caution' (Lewis 2003).

On a more positive note, it should be stated that wide coverage of health issues in features pages and broadcast documentary and magazine programmes may help people to lead healthier lives. Although features are less likely than news to influence policy-makers, they are an increasingly important source of information and advice for the public.

News and features

There is clearly a difference between the functions – and influence – of news and features in the media. Media theorist Denis McQuail argues that the distinction goes to the heart of modern notions of journalistic objectivity:

> *'News' is expected to consist of relevant and verifiable facts about actual and significant circumstances and events (recent or ongoing). The conventions underpinning this expectation are largely shared by news sources, journalists and audiences. Key elements are the separation of fact from opinion and the claim to be 'truth'. Features, by contrast, do not have any single definition and deviate on one or more of the characteristics mentioned. Despite the factuality expectation, news is also open to differential framing and presentation that can influence its effects. Features are diverse and diffuse in their reach and impact. For these reasons would-be influencers have sought to gain access to news or to adopt strategies of news management that further their goals.*

(McQuail, personal communication 2003)

In general, our research appears to confirm that – while newspaper news coverage of health issues tends to replicate the emphases and absences found in broadcast news – the narrowest and most extreme representations of health (in story choice, not necessarily in tone and content) appear in broadcast bulletins with a remit to concentrate on the main stories of the day. As we shall hear from BBC executives later (*see* Section 4), this polarisation of news topics is seen as almost inevitable. News bulletins on radio and television cannot be expected to match the spread of news and topical features that tend to provide a more balanced coverage across the pages of newspapers.

Media theorists argue that it is news rather than features material that does most to influence governments and shape public opinion (Holland 1998). According to McQuail (personal communication 2003), as far as influence is concerned, news has several advantages. In particular, he cites: 'the higher claim to being true and the greater trust it engenders, its immediacy and impact, plus the fact that national media of all kinds tend to recognise and disseminate the same news or at least provide news about the same main events, thus contributing to a shared "agenda" of what is significant.'

Although feature coverage undoubtedly helps to influence a climate of opinion, it does not have the same impact on agendas as a running news story repeated regularly across outlets. Opinions really start to shift when a story breaks in the newspapers, is taken up in television and radio programmes and carried over to the next day's papers. This underlines the importance of newspaper news, rather than features, for setting policy agendas, and the greater value of news rather than features to those who want to influence policy decisions. Paradoxically, however, as McQuail points out, the power of news to influence depends on audiences expecting it to have some immunity from manipulation and propaganda. The more the latter are practised, the less news is trusted and the less influence it is likely to have.

Influencing policy

One does not have to look far for signs that policy-makers believe in the power of the media. Politicians schedule their announcements, whenever possible, to meet news deadlines. They judge their own performance – and are judged by their colleagues – by the amount of favourable or unfavourable media attention they receive. The Blair Government is well known for its careful attention to media management. Cabinet ministers who receive a consistently bad press tend not to last long in the job. Broadly speaking, policy-makers care what the media say for two reasons. First, because they believe the media may both reflect and influence public opinion. Second, because the media generate debates and conversations among political elites that, in turn, influence the way power is exercised. Third, because policy-makers' own fortunes at the ballot box, their opportunities for preferment and the chances of their party staying in or entering government are seen as depending, to a large degree, on how they are portrayed in the media and how their words and actions are reported by them.

It is harder to find clear evidence of direct influence of news reporting on policy-making, because the process is subject to a range of other influences, including economic factors, global developments, electoral cycles, political opportunism and even research findings. One example, though, could be the campaign by the *Sun* against restrictions on duty-free tobacco. Following the campaign, there was a rise in duty-free tobacco allowances, prompting jubilant headlines: 'Ferry rush after *Sun*'s victory on cheap cigs' (*Sun*, 31 October 2002). In the article beneath the headline, a spokeswoman for the P&O ferry company was quoted as saying: 'The *Sun*'s victory has had an immediate impact.' This victory will, according to cancer specialist Professor Richard Peto, inevitably lead to an increase in deaths as the deterrent effect of price on smokers is lost (personal communication).

Department of Health officials who took part in our interviews have confirmed that patterns of media coverage in the late 1990s helped to shape, or at least reinforce, Government policy on the NHS. Relentless media denigration of the NHS in the winter of 1999/2000 and heightened public concern (fuelled by a succession of stories about the winter 'crisis') was followed by a massive injection of new money into the NHS and the major reform programme set out in *The NHS Plan* (Department of Health 2000).

At no time during that period did the media pay any sustained attention to public health issues such as the impact of poverty, poor housing, social exclusion, smoking, diet and exercise, even though these might have delivered health benefits at far lower cost than improvements to the NHS. Public health came low on the agenda of *The NHS Plan* – forming Chapter 13 – and seems to have remained a second-order issue. Only once, in November 2002, did the then Secretary of State for Health, Alan Milburn, deliver a major statement on public health. His speech promised stronger health warnings on cigarette packets and a ban on 'misleading double-speak', for example, terms such as 'light' cigarettes. He said he was also considering 'payment by results' schemes for NHS trusts that met targets on cutting deaths from smoking, heart disease and cancer, and on reducing infant mortality. Most newspapers reported the speech, but the broadcast media – to Milburn's manifest regret – largely ignored it. The story did not feature on BBC television's *Ten O'Clock News*, on *Newsnight*, on Radio 5 Live's *8.00am News* or on Radio 4's *Today* programme. Little has happened since to suggest that public health is moving up the Government's agenda. Whether

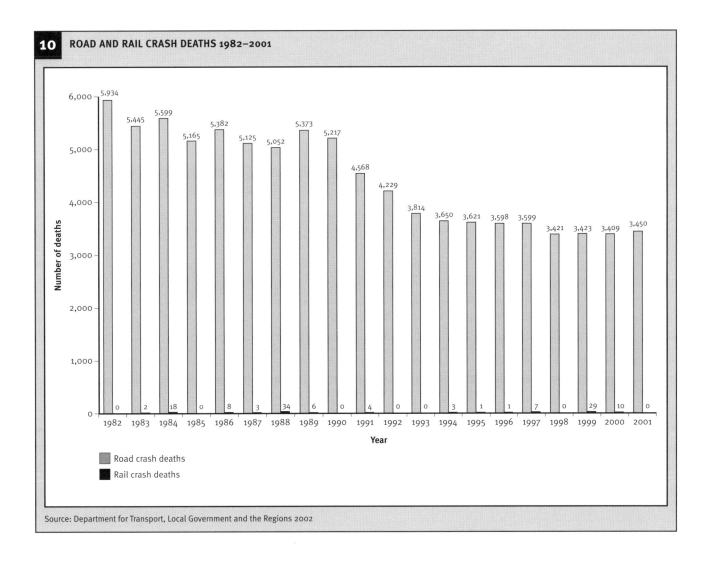

10 **ROAD AND RAIL CRASH DEATHS 1982–2001**

Source: Department for Transport, Local Government and the Regions 2002

the Government would have given public health higher priority if the media took more notice remains an open question.

The media can influence health-related policy in other subtle ways that sometimes lead to adverse consequences. Reporting of transport policy is one example. Travellers in a car are nearly six times more likely to die on the roads than travellers on the railways (Department of the Environment, Transport and Regions 2000), while total deaths per year from road accidents are, on average, 500 times higher than deaths from rail crashes (Department for Transport, Local Government and the Regions 2002). *See* Fig 10, above. Nevertheless, road accidents and road deaths – because they are seen as routine – fail to attract anything like the degree of media attention paid to (relatively rare) railway accidents.

There are several reasons for this imbalance.
- The high but flat curve of the road crash graph renders the story inherently uninteresting to journalists, while infrequent but spectacular train crashes create spikes of news interest.
- People feel, rightly or wrongly, that they are in control of their own risks when they are on the road.
- Rail safety has become a metaphor for the perceived lack of competence of rail managers.

Does this imbalance of news coverage influence policy? The Government is now in the process of installing a safety system called the Train Protection and Warning System (TPWS) on the railways that will cost £10 million for every death averted (Railway Safety 2002). The Government valuation for preventing a fatality on the roads is £1.14 million. Local authorities say they can save a life on the roads for as little as £100,000, but do not have enough staff to put safety improvements in place. Robert Gifford of the Parliamentary Advisory Council on Transport Safety (PACTS) says this is a gross imbalance in Government spending, fuelled partly by media hype over rail crashes (personal communication 2002). The Transport Select Committee on Speed complained in 2002 that some newspapers that championed rail safety were at the same time undermining road safety by campaigning against speed humps and safety cameras (Transport Select Committee on Speed 2002).

The BBC's Transport Correspondent, Simon Montague, told a conference in 2003: 'It can be argued that there is a huge distortion in the political, public and media response to casualties on the railways, compared with those on other forms of transport. It raises the key question of whether the proportion of safety spending invested in rail is truly to the best overall benefit of society, in terms of saving the most life across all transport modes' (Montague 2003).

This imbalance of media coverage of transport risks may have an indirect effect on health. If Government investment in road safety remains at a relatively low level, children are more likely to be denied the freedom to travel unaccompanied by parents concerned about speeding cars. As child inactivity has increased, so has obesity, which is predicted to lead to more diabetes, early blindness, cancer and heart attacks. Children who spend little time walking or running will fail to lay down sufficient bone mass – a development that could lead to higher demands for hip replacements in later life. Professor Philip James of the International

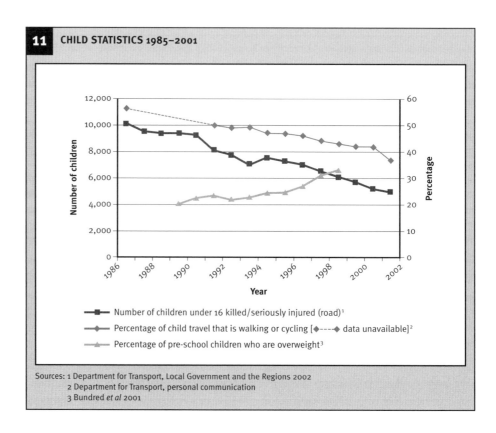

11 CHILD STATISTICS 1985–2001

Year

—■— Number of children under 16 killed/seriously injured (road)[1]
—◆— Percentage of child travel that is walking or cycling [◆----◆ data unavailable][2]
—▲— Percentage of pre-school children who are overweight[3]

Sources: 1 Department for Transport, Local Government and the Regions 2002
2 Department for Transport, personal communication
3 Bundred et al 2001

Obesity Taskforce observed that newspapers that had professed a concern about obesity had actively campaigned against measures designed to make roads less hostile to walking and cycling, which improve health (James 2003). *See* Fig 11, opposite.

The watchdog function

Disproportionate patterns of news reporting may have adverse consequences for health-related public behaviour and policy-making. But sometimes media alerts prove beneficial, when the media sound the alarm about health risks that have been underestimated or denied by experts or policy-makers. As noted earlier, by publicising the risks posed to human health by 'mad cow' disease, the media prompted the Government to stop denying that there was any danger and take steps to avoid risks to human health. This was a case of the media acting in the public interest by holding the Government to account – an essential part of the democratic process. There have been – and will be in future – other instances where a genuine risk is necessarily exposed, to influence behaviour and policy, in the public interest.

Conclusion

The way health risks are reported may sometimes alert people and governments to genuine risks and prompt appropriate action. However, in other cases, news media coverage may encourage people to change their behaviour in ways that are not in their own best health interests, or it may prevent them from adopting healthier lifestyles. It may deter authorities from taking more proactive measures to protect health, or lead to changes in policy with unforeseen negative consequences. From a public health perspective, then, news matters.

4 The journalists' responses

Following our analysis of media content, we explored journalists' own interpretations and explanations about patterns of media reporting of health issues. We asked news reporters and editors to respond to the comments of public health experts and policy-makers and to the results of our survey. The main areas of criticism were that the media under-reported some important health risks and over-reported others that were less important, and that they did not act sufficiently in their audiences' best interests. We interviewed senior journalists from the BBC, *The Guardian* and the *Daily Mirror* (*see* Appendix). The *Daily Mail* declined to comment. However, we interviewed journalists on the *Daily Mail* who agreed to give a personal view.

Several key themes emerged from our interviews and these are explored below.

Why news reporting should not reflect health risks

Broadly, our interviewees found the results of our survey intriguing and provocative. They typically had an idea of how news priorities compared across the industry, but few had seen their performance reflected back in this way. Some were surprised that they had covered one type of story so much and covered others much less, and indicated that the research might prompt them to seek out more stories that would help to prevent ill health. But all drew a clear distinction between their job and the role of public health protagonists. Niall Dickson, the BBC's Social Affairs Editor, summed up: 'We are not chroniclers of society. We are not doing a sociological thesis, not attempting to shape public opinion. We report the news. News is what is interesting – it is what people talk about in the pub.'

Richard Sambrook, the BBC's Director of News, rejected the suggestion that there should be 'a direct correlation between what kills people and what gets covered'. This was not, he said, the purpose of news.

Many of our interviewees were wary of the notion that news agendas could be challenged from the outside. News, they felt, was more of an art than a science, reliant on the finely honed instincts of the editor of the day. Decisions on difficult issues were taken quickly, often under pressure of deadlines and on a story-by-story basis. They gave a range of reasons why some stories were presented as 'news' and others were not. It was certainly a flexible concept. Mark Georgiou of the BBC *6 O'Clock News* said: 'News is what my editor says it is. And when I am duty editor, it is what I say it is.'

Why stories are selected

News is contingent. A story that could lead the paper on a slow news day might not merit a single paragraph on a busy day. This level of relativity is difficult to understand for professionals working in cultures with more absolute values. What becomes 'news' depends partly on how hot the competition is for available space. Pressure comes not only from the length of the bulletin or number of available news pages, but from the number of story sources – lobby groups, Government departments, experts, etc – trying to get into the news. Competition is more intense around news outlets considered to be of high status and especially influential.

Television news programmes have been confirmed in a survey for the Independent Television Commission to be the major purveyor of news to the public (Hargreaves and James 2002). The BBC's *Ten O'Clock News* was under more extreme pressure than the other BBC outlets in our survey from those trying to influence the agenda – not just on health but on a wide range of topics. Mark Popescu, Editor of the *Ten O'Clock News*, told us he had been asked by BBC managers to give more coverage to 18 different story areas, including China, East Asia, Eastern Europe and business news. 'We never get asked to do less on anything,' he observed.

The hotter the competition, the higher the premium placed on novelty and drama. This did not bode especially well for a range of stories about major health risks.

Jill Palmer, Health Correspondent for the *Daily Mirror* since 1985, described her efforts to get stories about mental health into the paper: 'I think it's a fascinating area, with so many people affected by mental health problems, but there's not much interest here. The editors say "you did something on that last month". In the tabloids, mental health is only sexy for the wrong reasons – if there's a violent attack or something.'

Mark Popescu described his role as being a selector of stories. There were always scores of stories running 'in the news' on any given day, he told us. His job was to pick the ones that were of greatest significance; the role was primarily reactive, not proactive. That often meant picking up stories from the press.

Several of our interviewees pointed to the *Daily Mail* as a powerful source of 'news' for other newspapers and for broadcast news. Its campaign against the MMR vaccine was cited as an irresistible story that had to be pursued as 'news'. Popescu said the controversy over MMR would continue across the media as long as the *Daily Mail* kept running with the story. If issues were opened up to public debate by widely read newspapers, he said, he was obliged to consider running them on his bulletin.

The *Daily Mail*'s campaign was not the only factor affecting coverage of the MMR story, however. Nor did scientific evidence alone justify the scale of coverage the story received. According to Popescu, an item became a big news story when it began to resonate across different news media and in Whitehall. 'Strictly on the level of risk, we probably over-reported MMR,' he said, 'but I am not just governed by that cold calculation. I am also governed by whether there is a public debate going on, whether the Government is involved, whether the Chief Medical Officer is involved and whether things are being said by all of those people, which I have a responsibility to report as well.'

Unsurprisingly, good pictures and strong human interest angles boosted a story's chances of getting into the 'news'. According to many of our interviewees, preventive health measures were under-reported partly because journalists liked to tell health stories through the experiences of individual victims – while preventive health tends to focus on how to prevent people from becoming victims. Sickness and the treatment of it were far more attractive to editors than nebulous notions about disease prevention, by its nature hard to quantify or to identify with tangible – or reportable – outcomes. Mark Popescu conceded that preventive medicine was 'not terribly well covered in mainstream news'.

Major stories could move in and out of the media spotlight without their actual importance to health diminishing. This may be a matter of timing, or of changing patterns of news management. Jill Palmer pointed to the role of the Department of Health in proactive news-making, and to the importance of personal contact between ministers and journalists. She told us she used to do a lot of stories on public health partly because she knew Tessa Jowell (Minister for Public Health in 1997/8). Now, she heard much less about public health from the department's press office; public health was no less important, but she nevertheless found there were fewer stories to write.

HIV/AIDS was once a huge news story, but now it rarely makes the headlines, although it remains a significant risk to health. Journalists could claim with some justification that the spread of AIDS would have been much worse without the extent of media coverage it received in the 1980s. But, as Niall Dickson, the BBC's Social Affairs Editor, told us, now that the novelty had worn off, it would take an exceptional event to push AIDS back onto the agenda. 'In the early days, we were providing public information. That is, I guess, about changing behaviour, so you can't deny that's part of your role. But once it stops being a news story and everybody knows about it then I think that moves on to being someone else's responsibility.'

Many of our interviewees claimed that stories that couldn't compete successfully for news space could just as well be covered in the features pages, or in documentary or magazine programmes. Richard Sambrook, Director of BBC News, said that if the *Ten O'Clock News* had not covered a particular story about mental health, it didn't mean the BBC had ignored the issue; mental health would almost certainly have been covered in other kinds of BBC programme, he said.

Several newspaper journalists said they used features pages to promote stories about healthy living. James Meikle, Health Correspondent on *The Guardian*, told us he thought food and health were very important and had been the province of the tabloids for too long. 'I like featurey lifestyle pieces about diet. I am particularly interested in getting original stuff in that's not in the news.'

The influence of institutional and personal values

Many of the journalists' reasons for selecting 'news' were common to all news media: novelty, drama, 'running stories' that resonate widely, strong visuals, human interest, news management, and timing. But our interviewees also made it clear that there were significant variations among and between newspapers and broadcast programmes. Different institutional values led to widely differing approaches to the same story. The BBC, for example, had a sense of its obligations as a public service broadcaster to provide objective reporting that served the public interest. Statutory regulation also influenced the broadcasters' agendas.

The BBC News directorate had recognised that intense competition for airtime on the *Ten O'Clock News* could lead to important stories being excluded, and told us it offered guidelines to help increase its story count on under-reported topics. Richard Sambrook suggested he was open to the idea of proactive news gathering, but at the same time was adamant that the BBC should avoid accusations of 'campaigning', because this was not consistent with the BBC's charter. Sambrook acknowledged, however, that what constituted campaigning journalism was something of a grey area. Pursuit of original stories on a little-reported topic might be dismissed as a campaign, but the alternative might be to follow up stories initiated by newspapers that had no such reservations about campaigning journalism.

Jill Palmer of the *Daily Mirror* suggested that decisions on how to cover the NHS were influenced by newspapers' political allegiances. 'When the Tories were in charge, the *Mirror* were running NHS crisis stories all the time. Recently we don't run so many. That's partly because we're a Labour paper and Labour are in power, but partly because we don't get so many stories about things going wrong. I think that things probably are genuinely better than they were. The *Mail* is interested in NHS crisis stories for the same reason as we were in the 80s. It's a good way to get at the Government.' James Meikle, of the left-leaning *Guardian*, told us he was not interested in crisis stories unless they illustrated a systemic failure. 'Individuals make mistakes and the NHS is a huge organisation, so I don't want to report blunders all the time because blunders will happen.'

The fact that politics plays a more obvious role in news selection in the press than in the broadcast media could be attributed at least partly to the role of the broadcasting regulators.

Institutional values affected the way news media reported 'health scares'. According to Mark Popescu, the BBC's *Ten O'Clock News* team would have lengthy discussions about whether a scare story should run at all, and, if so, where in the bulletin it should go. 'There are many health "scare stories" which come up that don't actually make it. The first thing you do is ask: "Is it accurate? Is it factual? What's the research base? What are the reputations of the people who did the research? Is it new?" People may be surprised to know how seriously we debate these issues.'

From another perspective, scandals or scare stories forged links between journalists and their outraged publics. Chris Shaw, Head of News and Current Affairs at Channel 5, commented, in a report published recently by the Independent Television Commission, that his station's biggest audience response came when they were exposing something new or outrageous (like a health scare) (Hargreaves and James 2002). This public response, measured in letters, emails and phone calls, provided a powerful affirmation to some editors that they had touched their audiences, and motivated them to seek other examples of the types of stories that could create this level of response.

Different again was the view from the *Daily Mail*. Asked about the paper's handling of the MMR scare, our contact (who asked not to be named) described a sense of obligation to individual readers, but not to the public at large. 'It is not our job to promote group immunity. If some of our readers' kids might be affected as individuals – even if that is a remote chance – then we have to report it, and will continue to do so.' The *Mail* was interested in 'strong stories that would have a resonance with its readers', our contact said. 'Some of these might appear to be scare stories – but if they have a certain basis in science, they make news. Our readers are adults and they can decide for themselves how scared they ought to be. Of course in empirical terms we do go over the top from time to time – and there might be all sorts of reasons for that … but if people didn't like the paper's coverage they wouldn't buy it.' Another *Daily Mail* journalist offered another rationale. 'Health scares are part of the price you pay for an open, democratic society in which a free press plays a crucial part.'

The values and preferences of individual reporters also influenced the selection of news. The *Daily Mirror*'s Jill Palmer told us she felt a personal responsibility to try to get stories into the paper that gave people advice about their own health. 'I am interested in smoking, especially as I have a teenage daughter. But it's hard to find new angles. If I can find some real news, I'll write the story.'

Asked about the preponderance of stories about breast cancer, and the relative neglect of prostate cancer – an equally serious health risk – James Meikle, Health Correspondent of *The Guardian*, told us: 'It's partly an instinctive thing. Journalists are people, and many of us know women who've had breast cancer – I'm sure that influences what we write about. But cancer is a gut reaction thing. I think on the whole we probably do too many cancer stories, compared with other diseases.'

Some individuals saw it as their duty to allay public fears on particular issues. Others felt it was their role as public guardians to highlight scare stories, as long as the facts were strong enough to warrant a degree of genuine concern. Jill Palmer said she regularly ran reassuring pieces about MMR: 'Why is it that when the MMR vaccine is given all round the world, we alone in Britain are worried about it? If it was so bad, someone would have sued in America, where it is mandatory.' The BBC's Niall Dickson generally supported that view, but counselled keeping an open mind while the science remained uncertain. 'It is true that from time to time there are mavericks who are right and the establishment is entirely wrong.'

Unsurprisingly, the personal values of individual journalists tended to be in line with those of their employing organisation. We came across entirely different attitudes on BSE and AIDS stories between our *Daily Mirror* and *Guardian* interviews. This seemed to reflect a combination of personal interests, editorial values and degrees of pressure on news space (with many more column inches in a broadsheet than in a tabloid). According to Jill Palmer: 'AIDS has dropped out of the news because the deaths time-bomb that was predicted never happened.' James Meikle said that *The Guardian* still took a strong interest in AIDS stories, particularly in the availability of drugs in Africa and the role of the big pharmaceutical companies. And while Jill Palmer declared: 'BSE is boring', James Meikle said he thought the issue was still very much alive. 'It is not clear to me that the authorities have dealt with all the fall-out, like infected blood, quarantining surgical instruments and so on. There will be more stories on this, I'm sure.' Some journalists attest that there is a market in scaring people. As Chris Birkett, Executive Producer of Sky News, remarked at a recent conference on media and risk: 'The audience appears to want to be scared.'

Risk psychology helps to explain why journalists bias their stories against the public health professionals' views of risk, either deliberately to appeal to the public, or accidentally by painting vivid pictures of risks in words, sounds or television images. Although some science correspondents have received a scientific training, most journalists have not. Therefore they may tend to make judgements in ways that are similar to their own lay audiences – and very differently from those of health professionals. As we discussed in Section 3, lay audiences are more likely to respond to risks intuitively than with actuarial precision.

Indeed, many of our journalist interviewees admitted that they did not give a great deal of thought to what impact their risk stories might have on the public, as news was itself a largely intuitive business, and it was not the responsibility of journalists to predict the consequences of their reporting of 'news'.

Conclusion

There was no disagreement among the journalists we interviewed about the findings of our research – that some important health risks were under-reported while other, relatively minor, risks were over-reported, and that news agendas favoured stories about the NHS over stories about health. Nevertheless, all our interviewees seemed to think that – in one way or another – they were serving the public interest in the way they reported health issues. With the exception of some BBC personnel, they rarely reflected on how or why they favoured some categories of health story over others, or whether they could or should do things differently. Some were prepared to consider alternatives. Most indicated that existing news priorities were non-negotiable. The balance of news reporting on health issues was attributed to a variety of factors. Some selection criteria were shared between all news outlets; others varied according to institutional values and the personal interests of individual reporters and editors. By and large, journalists respond to health risks in ways that are more akin to lay audiences than to health professionals.

5 Ways ahead

Could things be different?

It would be unrealistic to expect radical change. However, it is possible to envisage a less entrenched stand-off and more understanding between public health protagonists and the media. This would require a shift on both sides: journalists having the goodwill to challenge their own assumptions, and the experts and politicians developing more flair in presenting their material.

The journalists

Starting with the journalists, four observations arise from this study. The first is about broadening agendas. More reporters and editors should be more willing to acknowledge that 'news' is largely constructed by the media themselves. Issues that rank high on news agendas are not always there because they are new but because media producers consider them important and of interest to audiences. The fact that they are featured in the 'news' helps to make them seem important and interesting, so that they invite further media interest. There are areas where significant new developments occur, but which are largely ignored by the news media – sometimes to the detriment of public health. Stories that could add to people's knowledge about health and help to promote better health are there to be found.

Second, more could be done to improve the way risks are reported. Although reporters and editors in the national media usually work to high standards of factual accuracy, more care could be taken to put emotive visual material and human-interest stories in perspective, showing the scale and relative severity of the risks involved. A particular pitfall for non-specialist journalists is the potential confusion between degrees of risk and how these are conveyed.

Third, there could be more reflection on the cumulative effect on public perceptions of risk of 'running stories' and continuing silences. Editors and reporters make fresh judgements each day about the value and ranking of stories. They do not always have a chance to stand back and consider how stories build, or fail to build, or how the weight of their reporting accumulates. Yet it is the impact over time of patterns of reporting that is most likely to influence policy-making and public behaviour. Such a change would require a depth of self-analysis that many news organisations would not consider necessary or perhaps even appropriate.

A fourth observation concerns the BBC. As a public service broadcaster, it strives to present information even-handedly and to play the honest broker between sources of data and knowledge and its audiences. To avoid accusations of bias or campaigning, BBC news programmes often feel obliged to stick with the mainstream news agenda – an agenda partly constructed by newspapers that may have strong campaigning interests of their own. The BBC could arguably better fulfil its public service obligations if it initiated more stories and showed greater scepticism about the agenda of newspapers.

The public health specialists

Moving on to the public health protagonists, our first observation here is that they could benefit from a better understanding of how news agendas are developed, the imperatives and constraints under which different media outlets operate, and why some health stories are more likely to resonate with editors than others. It may be fair to argue that news coverage should pay more attention to proven health risks, but it is also important to accept that we meddle with editorial autonomy at our peril. Media freedom is widely agreed to be an essential underpinning of democracy. And – more mundanely – a proportionate match between news coverage and health risks would make programmes and papers so boring that no-one would pay attention to them.

If news stories are always constructed, then the experts and politicians can play their part in the building work. Skilful handling of information and argument, with attention paid to sounds and pictures where appropriate, can help the media to absorb new and different stories and angles into their news agendas. It is also useful to distinguish the roles and potential impact of news and features in the media. Feature material may help to influence public behaviour. News is more likely to influence policy-makers.

The policy-makers

Policy-makers concerned with health issues might ask themselves more often whether newspapers and bulletins are reflecting public opinion or merely trying to influence it. For instance, as some journalists have pointed out, a 'feeding frenzy' in the media can be created by a newspaper campaign that is taken up by television, inviting comments from opinion formers, including Government ministers, which invite further headlines. All of this can create a sense of urgency among the political classes without having any firm basis in public opinion.

Communication of risk

More generally, it may be helpful on all sides to reflect on different ways of communicating and interpreting risk. There may well be room for news media to improve the way they communicate risks associated with certain health hazards, for instance through more robust handling of data analysis, ratios and percentages. At the same time, it is important to understand how audiences interpret risk and how emotional responses can override rational calculations – and how different kinds of interpretations can be triggered by different approaches to communication. Evocative pictures of children in distress, for instance, are likely to overwhelm the effects of statistics demonstrating relative risks.

Why some sources are considered trustworthy and others less so is also highly relevant to this debate. Trust grows out of mutual understanding and respect. These qualities are not always evident in political relationships, where governments and their advisors have often tended to treat citizens as though they cannot be relied upon to respond in a mature fashion to complex or uncomfortable information and must be shielded from it with half-truths or denials. Once the media get a whiff of a cover-up, headlines are guaranteed and may precipitate a full-scale panic, suggesting an even greater risk than the one the Government is trying to play down. There are signs that the Government has learned from the mistakes of the past and is adopting a more transparent approach to risk communication. This trend should be encouraged.

It might help the debate over health risks if there were more effective advocacy for public health, to help raise the profile of issues other than NHS 'crises' and disproportionate scare stories. It is beyond the scope of this paper to consider ways of building more effective public health advocacy. However, it may be argued that the media pay relatively little attention to public health because the people with most power and influence in the health system appear to be primarily concerned with health services rather than with health. This appears true for the Secretary of State for Health, all but one junior minister in the Department of Health, and almost all NHS trust chairs and chief executives (not to mention the Prime Minister, who has given priority to reforming the NHS). Some public health protagonists argue that doctors, who are a prime source of stories for journalists, should be more proactive in speaking out about public health issues.

Signs of change

There are some signs of change that may possibly encourage a shift in the balance of risk and reporting. Within Government, there is growing awareness of the need to manage demands for health services (and thereby contain NHS costs) by preventing illness and developing a stronger capacity among individuals and communities to maintain their own health (Wanless 2002). If Government begins to attach more importance to public health, rather than the NHS, it may move higher up the news agenda. Primary care trusts, responding to Government targets and their own new responsibilities for population health, are beginning to be more attentive to health promotion and preventive medicine – with some evidence of early success on smoking cessation (Department of Health 2001) and prevention of premature death from heart disease (Office for National Statistics 2003). This may herald a move towards stronger advocacy for public health within the health system. Efforts are being made within the Department of Health and across Government to improve the way health risks are communicated (Cabinet Office Strategy Unit 2002; Bennett and Calman 1999; Petts and Homan 2000). Within the media, the BBC, following a seminar between BBC journalists and experts in risk, has drawn up draft guidance to help news reporters and editors improve their handling of risk stories (*see* box opposite), and there is more discussion than previously about news values and protocols, which indicates a growing awareness of these dilemmas.

BBC DRAFT RISK GUIDANCE FOR JOURNALISTS

- What exactly is the risk? How big is it? Who does it affect?
- How has the risk been measured? How big is the sample? Who funded the research? How reputable is the source?
- If you are reporting a relative risk, have you made clear what the baseline risk is (for example, a 100 per cent increase in a problem that affects one person in 2,000 will still affect only one in 1,000)?
- Have you asked 'How safe is this?' rather than 'Is this safe?'
- If a scientist or a victim is taking a view that runs against majority scientific opinion, is that clear in the report and in the casting of the discussion and subsequent questions?
- Have you told the audience how to find more information?
- Can you find a comparison to make the risk easier to understand (for example, it's as risky as drinking a pint of beer)?
- Have you given the audience information to put the risk in context (for example, women who stop taking the pill during a pill scare face worse risks from either abortion or childbirth)?
- Is the scale of reporting in proportion to the extent of the risk? Will our reporting increase or decrease risks in society?
- Can we use a story about a specific risk as a springboard to discuss other related risks (for example, train safety versus road safety)?

Source: BBC 2003 (developed following a seminar between BBC journalists and experts in risk).

It is to be hoped that as handling of risk issues by all parties continues to improve over time, the public will learn to live with uncertainties, rather than expecting governments or experts to have ready answers to everything and the perfect antidote to every health hazard. For this to happen there needs to be a sustained public debate about how to understand and negotiate health risks, and how to achieve a closer match between proven health risks and news coverage, without compromising media freedom. This paper is intended to stimulate and support that debate.

Appendix: Methodology

Our intention was to examine the claims frequently made by health professionals that the news media do not adequately cover major risks to public health, but focus instead on trivial risks, diverting viewers and readers away from serious threats to their health, and creating health scares.

Before our analysis of news, we sought the opinions of leading public health and health policy specialists about the coverage of health issues in the media. We discussed patterns of media coverage of health and the importance of the media in shaping health policy, and discussed how readers and viewers might understand and use the information presented to them. We conducted ten interviews with leading public health professionals and six interviews with politicians and policy specialists with interests in health. Following our news analysis, we interviewed six leading journalists from all but one of the media we studied (the exception was the *Daily Mail*, which declined to comment). We showed them our news analysis results and asked them to comment on and explain the results we had found, suggest some of the ways they felt audiences responded to health stories and discuss how stories are made. All the interviews were recorded and transcribed.

News analysis

In order to investigate coverage of health risks in the news, we selected three BBC news programmes for a year-long analysis and three daily, national newspapers for a three-month analysis.

BBC programmes

We selected three BBC news programmes for their leading position within the BBC and for their different predicted audiences. The *Ten O'Clock News* aims at a large (about one million), mainly well-informed audience. It covers what are judged to be the top stories of the day, with some analysis on the leading items. (We analysed the *Nine O'Clock News* until 4 October 2000 when the *Ten O'Clock News* began broadcasting.) The format of *Newsnight* enables much more in-depth discussion of a few selected stories each night, and Radio 5 Live's *8.00am News* carries a few informative, news-in-brief-style stories aimed at a wide audience with differing social and educational backgrounds. Our year-long analysis of the BBC ran from 10 September 2000 to 10 September 2001. This time frame was selected in order to avoid the aftermath of September 11 when all news output focused on international events rather than on domestic news.

For all three programmes we examined daily output, including running orders and scripts, using BBC electronic archives. A total of 540 stories concerning health and health issues were copied and later coded, depending on the main focus of the story. Our coding criteria were resolved after preliminary examinations of the news output, and according to our original research interests. We redeveloped the coding until we were adequately able to capture all the health stories.

19 CODING CATEGORIES

Smoking Stories about the health effects of smoking, giving up smoking and debates about tax on cigarettes

Alcohol Stories about health effects of alcohol, cutting down, alcohol policy, changes in alcohol consumption, crime, accidents and alcohol, and celebrities drinking

Obesity Stories about the health effects of obesity, changes in national rates of obesity and how to lose weight

Public health Stories about public health programmes from public health bodies, eg, advice on getting flu jabs

MMR Stories about the MMR, links to autism and incidence of measles

BSE/vCJD Stories about rates and incidence of BSE and vCJD, and effects of and changes to Government policy

Health news Stories about people getting ill including, for example, the incidence of meningitis and TB. Not including health scare and health care stories

Female cancers Stories about cancers specific to women

Male cancers Stories about cancers specific to men

NHS in crisis Stories about the NHS in crisis, including waiting lists, lack of funding, closures, etc

Negligence Stories about negligence and misconduct from NHS staff

Politics Stories about the politics of the NHS, including party political issues

NHS information Stories about the NHS (not crisis, negligence or politics) including wage rates, new hospitals and services changes in NHS staff structures

Treatment Information about new research and existing treatments for a variety of medical conditions

Shipman Stories about Harold Shipman

HIV/AIDS Stories about HIV/AIDS including treatments, rates, politics and drug availability (including international)

Ethics Stories about ethical debates around health care, intervention, drug availability and research. For example, separation of conjoined twins, right to die and research on foetal material

Mental health Stories about mental health issues. Including rates, incidence, research, treatment, care, and crimes related to mental health problems

Complementary medicine Stories about complementary medicine including treatments, research, individual case studies and regulation of practitioners and treatments

Having undertaken a detailed analysis of the news using 19 different coding categories, we merged some of these categories into an eightfold schema in order to differentiate primarily between health care, health scare and general health news stories (*see* box below). For this analysis we grouped the three BBC news programmes together. This enabled us to draw from our preliminary analysis and reveal some of the broader underlying trends in health coverage. We repeated this procedure for newspapers.

---

8 CODING CATEGORIES

1: Proven health risks
Smoking
Alcohol
Obesity
Public health

2: Health scares
MMR
BSE/vCJD

3: Health news
Female cancers
Male cancers

4: Health care stories
NHS in crisis
Negligence
Politics
NHS information
Treatment
Harold Shipman

5: HIV/AIDS

6: Ethics

7: Mental health

8: Complementary therapies

Newspapers

We decided to examine three months of health coverage in the *Daily Mirror*, the *Daily Mail* and *The Guardian*. The papers were selected because of their different political stance, their differing readership and political importance. We examined all health stories in all three papers for three months from October to December 2002; the research was conducted in January and February 2003. We used an almost identical coding sheet for newspapers and the BBC but as there were no stories about Harold Shipman during our three-month period we excluded that category. There were over 1,351 health stories in the three papers during our three-month period (*see* box, opposite), providing, we felt, an adequate sample to allow us some interesting insights into coverage of health in newspapers. We also separated 'features' stories about health and 'news' stories about health; we felt that 'news' and 'features' have differing impacts upon their audiences and certainly 'news' articles are taken more seriously and read more fully by other media practitioners, policy-makers and politicians. Our results reveal that there are indeed substantive differences in type and style of story carried in the features and news sections of all three papers. We then recoded our stories using the eightfold schema we had used for the BBC, allowing us to produce a broad-scale analysis of newspaper coverage.

NUMBER OF STORIES

	Health risks				Health scares		Health news			
	Smoking	Alcohol	Obesity	Public health	MMR	BSE/vCJD	Health news	Female cancers	Male cancers	NHS in crisis
BBC	14	7	4	10	12	60	43	16	4	58
Newspaper news	27	39	13	47	8	27	126	21	2	46
Newspaper features	22	151	51	8	18	25	15	66	21	63
TOTALS	**63**	**197**	**68**	**65**	**38**	**112**	**184**	**103**	**27**	**167**

	Health care Stories					HIV/AIDS	Ethics	Mental health	Comple-mentary	TOTAL
	Negligence	Politics	NHS information	Treatment	Shipman					
BBC	52	28	20	75	11	23	93	9	1	**540**
Newspaper news	61	48	37	104	0	20	35	8	12	**681**
Newspaper features	6	37	46	1	0	53	4	78	5	**670**
TOTALS	**119**	**113**	**103**	**180**	**11**	**96**	**132**	**95**	**18**	**1,891**

Following our analysis of patterns of health coverage in the media, we produced a 'deaths per story' chart for each media outlet. These charts portray the number of deaths per story for smoking, alcohol, obesity, measles, vCJD, AIDS and mental disorders. The charts are intended to test our preliminary thesis about 'proportionality': that the media over-report trivial risks to health and under-report major threats to health such as smoking, alcohol, obesity and mental health problems. We divided the number of annual deaths in the UK from each health issue by the number of stories about that issue in our media outlets.

MORTALITY BY CATEGORY

	UK figures
Smoking	120,000[1]
Alcohol	33,000[2]
Obesity	30,000[3]
vCJD	20[4]
Measles	3[5]
AIDS/HIV	450[6] (AIDS deaths 2000)
Mental disorders	11,000[7] (Mortality)

Sources
1 ASH
2 Alcohol Concern Factsheet 18
3 National Audit Office Report
4 Department of Health 2001 figures
5 Department of Health 2000
6 Public Health Laboratory Services
7 National Statistics 1999 – Mental disorders included psychoses, senile and presenile organic psychotic conditions, alcohol dependence syndrome.

Thus the larger the resultant figure, the less coverage that issue gets per death. For example *Newsnight* has 60,000 deaths per story for smoking compared with 0.9 for BSE/vCJD for our period.

Interviewees

Public health specialists

Dr Harry Burns – Director of Public Health, Greater Glasgow Health Board
Professor Sir Richard Doll CH FRS – former Regis Professor, Oxford University
Andrew Dougal – Chief Executive, Northern Ireland Chest, Heart and Stroke
  Association
Professor Siân Griffiths – President, Faculty of Public Health Medicine
Dr Philip Harrison – Senior Medical Officer, Medical Research Council
Dr Desmond Julian – Emeritus Professor of Cardiology, University of Newcastle-
  upon-Tyne and formerly President of the British Cardiac Society
Professor Ragnar Lofstedt – Centre for Risk Management, King's College, London
Professor Mark McCarthy – Department of Epidemiology and Public Health,
  University College, London
Sir Richard Peto – Professor of Medical Statistics and Epidemiology, University
  of Oxford
Neville Rigby – Director of Policy and Public Affairs, International Obesity Taskforce

Politicians and advisors

Hazel Blears MP – Parliamentary Under Secretary of State for Public Health
Dr Liam Fox MP – Shadow Secretary of State for Health, Conservative Party
Dr Ian Gibson MP – Chair, House of Commons Select Committee for Science and
  Technology
Dr Evan Harris MP – Shadow Secretary of State for Health, Liberal Democratic Party
Two officials, Department of Health

Journalists

Chris Birkett, Executive Producer of Sky News
Niall Dickson – BBC Social Affairs Editor
James Meikle – Health Correspondent, *The Guardian*
Jill Palmer – Health Correspondent, the *Daily Mirror*
Mark Popescu – Editor, the *Ten O'Clock News*, BBC
Richard Sambrook – Director of BBC News

Others consulted

Professor John Adams – Department of Geography, University College, London
David Brindle – Editor, *Guardian Society*
Professor Jacquie Burgess – Professor of Geography, University College, London
Professor Andrew Evans – Centre for Transport Studies, University College, London
Mark Georgiou – Assistant Editor, *6 O'Clock News*, BBC
Robert Gifford – Director of Parliamentary Advisory Committee for Transport Safety
Professor Ian Hargreaves – Journalism, Cardiff University
Mayer Hillman – Senior Fellow Emeritus, Policy Studies Institute
Professor Tim Lang – Food Policy, Thames Valley University
Professor Denis McQuail – Emeritus Professor, Department of Communication,
  University of Amsterdam and Visiting Professor, Department of Politics,
  University of Southampton
Tony Taig – Risk Consultant, Director, TTAC

Bibliography

Adams J (1995). *Risk: The policy implications of risk compensation and plural rationalities*. London: UCL Press.

Allan S (2002). *Media, Risk and Science*. Milton Keynes: Open University Press.

Bennett P (1999). 'Understanding responses to risk: some basic findings' in *Risk Communication and Public Health*, Bennett P and Calman K eds, pp 3–20. Oxford: Oxford University Press.

Bennett P, Calman K eds (1999). *Risk Communication and Public Health*. Oxford: Oxford University Press.

Bundred P, Kitchiner D, Buchan I (2001). 'Prevalence of overweight and obese children between 1989–1998: population-based series of cross-sectional studies', 322:326. *British Medical Journal*.

Butler P (2002). 'Q&A: Measles and MMR'. Available at SocietyGuardian.co.uk

Cabinet Office Strategy Unit (2002). *Risk: Improving Government Capability to Handle Risk and Uncertainty*. London: Cabinet Office.

Department of the Environment, Transport and the Regions (2000). *Road Accidents Great Britain: 1999 – the Casualty Report*. London: The Stationery Office.

Department for Transport (2002). *Highways Economic Note Number 1*. London: Department for Transport.

Department for Transport, Local Government and the Regions (2002), *Transport Statistics Great Britain 2001*. London: The Stationery Office.

Department of Health (2001). *Statistics on smoking cessation services in the Health Action Zones in England, April 2000 to March 2001*, Bulletin 32. London: Office for National Statistics.

Department of Health (2000). *The NHS Plan*. London: Department of Health.

Food Standards Agency (2002). *Report of the Core Stakeholder Group on the Review of the Over-Thirty-Month Rule*, Annex 3, 3 July 2002.

Frewer LJ (1999). 'Public risk perceptions and risk communication' in *Risk Communication and Public Health*, Bennett P and Calman K eds, pp 21–33. Oxford: Oxford University Press.

Furedi F, Furedi A (1996). *The International Impact of a Pill Panic in the UK*. London: Birth Control Trust.

Hargreaves I, James J (2002). *New News, Old News*. London: ITC and BSC Research Publication.

Hargreaves I, Lewis J, Speers T (2003). *Towards a Better Map: Science, the public and the media*. Economic and Social Research Council Report.

Holland P (1998). 'The politics of the smile: "Soft news" and the sexualisation of the popular press' in *News, Gender and Power*, Carter C, Branston G and Allan S eds, pp 17–32. London: Blackwell.

James P (2003). Interview for the *Today* programme, 12 September.

Kitzinger J (1999). 'Researching risk and the media'. *Health, Risk and Society*, vol 1(1), pp 55–69.

Lawrie SM (2000). 'Newspaper coverage of psychiatric and physical illness'. *Psychiatric Bulletin*, vol 24, pp 104–6.

Lewis J (2003). 'Public duped by media over MMR'. Economic and Social Research Council Press Release, 29 May.

McQuail D (2002). *Mass Communication Theory*, 4th ed. London: Sage Publications.

Miller D, Macintyre S (1999). 'Risk communication: the relationship between the media, public beliefs and policy-making' in *Risk Communication and Public Health*, Bennett P and Calman K eds, pp 229–40. Oxford: Oxford University Press.

Montague S (2003). 'How TV and radio tackle transport stories', presented to the Transport and the Media Conference, The Centre for Transport Policy, Robert Gordon University, Aberdeen, 28 January. Unpublished.

Office for National Statistics (2003). *Health Statistics Quarterly 18*. London: Office for National Statistics.

Office for National Statistics (2002). *NHS Immunisation Statistics, England: 2001–2002. Bulletin 2002/18*. London: Office for National Statistics.

Office for National Statistics (1997). *Abortion Statistics: Series AB no.23*. London: Office for National Statistics.

Petts J, Homan J (2000). *Risk Literacy and the Public*. London: Department of Health.

Prime Minister's Speech (2001). 'Reform of Public Services', 16 July.

Railway Safety (2002). *Railway Group Safety Plan*. London: Railway Safety.

Riddell P (2003). 'Most voters have positive view of NHS, says poll'. *The Times*, 7 May, p 6.

Seale C (2002). *Media and Health*. London: Sage Publications.

Slovic P (2002). 'Risk as analysis and risk as feelings: some thoughts about affect, reason, risk and rationality'. Unpublished paper.

Slovic P (2000). *The Perception of Risk*. London: Earthscan.

Slovic P, Finucane M, Peters E, MacGregor DG (2002). 'The affect heuristic' in *Heuristics and Biases: The psychology of intuitive judgement*, Glovich T, Griffin D and Kahneman D eds, pp 397–426. Cambridge: Cambridge University Press.

Slovic P, Monahan J, MacGregor DG (2000). 'Violence, risk assessment and risk communication: the effects of using actual cases, providing instruction and employing probability versus frequency formats'. *Law and Human Behaviour*, vol 24(3), pp 271–96.

Transport Select Committee on Speed (2002). Minutes of evidence and appendices to 'Road Traffic Speed, Ninth Report of Transport, Local Government and the Regions', 13 June.

Wakefield AJ, Murch SH, Anthony A, Linnell J, Casson DM, Malik M, Berelowitz M, Dhillon AP, Thomson MA, Harvey P, Valentine A, Davies SA, Walker-Smith JA (1998). 'Ileal-lymphoid-nodular hyperplasia, non-specific colitis, and pervasive developmental disorder in children'. *Lancet*, vol 351, pp 637–41.

Wanless D (2002). *Securing our Future Health: Taking a long-term view*. London: HM Treasury.

Wellings K, Kane R (1999). 'Trends in teenage pregnancy in England and Wales: how can we explain them?' *Journal of the Royal Society of Medicine*, vol 92(6), pp 277–82.

Wood R, Botting B, Dunnell K (1997). 'Trends in conceptions before and after the 1995 pill scare'. *Population Trends*, vol 89, pp 5–12.